THE JOURNEY
OF
PERPETUAL
One Day at a Time

ANNIE FEENEY

The Journey of Perpetual
Copyright © 2025 Annie Feeney
Produced and printed by Stillwater River Publications.
All rights reserved. Written and produced in the United States of America. This book
may not be reproduced or sold in any form without the expressed, written permission
of the author and publisher.
Visit our website at www.StillwaterPress.com For more information.
First Stillwater River Publications Edition
ISBN: 978-1-965733-16-5
1 2 3 4 5 6 7 8 9 10
Written by Annie Feeney.
Published by Stillwater River Publications,
West Warwick, RI, USA.

Publisher's Cataloging-in-Publication
(Provided by Cassidy Cataloguing Services, Inc.)
Names: Feeney, Annie, author.
Title: The journey of Perpetual : one day at a time / Annie Feeney.
Identifiers: ISBN: 978-1-965733-16-5
Subjects: LCSH: Feeney, Annie. | Women sailors--United States--Biography. | Sail-
    ing--Atlantic Coast (U.S.) | Atlantic Coast (U.S.)--Description and travel. |
    LCGFT: Autobiographies. | Diaries. | BISAC: BIOGRAPHY & AUTOBI-
    OGRAPHY / Memoirs. | SPORTS & RECREATION / Water Sports /
    Sailing.
Classification: LCC: GV810.92.F44 A3 2025 | DDC: 797.124092--dc23

DEDICATION

I dedicate this memoir to my wife Ann Haas,
my navigator and true partner
who made this incredible journey our reality.

ACKNOWLEDGEMENTS

I would like to acknowledge our family and friends
who encouraged us along the way and
the amazing boating community who were always there
when we needed guidance or assistance.

BEFORE THE JOURNEY BEGAN

When my spouse, Ann, was offered a year-long sabbatical from City University of New York, where she had been a department chair, she had a plan. We would rent our houses, buy a sailboat, and live the year sailing. The amazing part of that plan was that she had been on a sailboat only twice in her life.

Not to be deterred, she enrolled in an on-the-water sailing course, and I accompanied her for support. Then, it was off to Atlantic City, New Jersey, for a weekend of various seminars and lectures, which included Sailing The Intracoastal Waterway, Women at the Helm, Outfitting a Sailboat, and basic navigation.

We found *Perpetual* in East Hampton, New York, and knew she was THE boat, a Pearson 28, big enough to live on and small enough to handle

I resigned from my nursing position in Westchester, New York, and voila, that's how the journey began.

THE JOURNEY OF *PERPETUAL*

ONE DAY AT A TIME

LEAVING CENTERPORT, NEW YORK

August 17, 1998

Day one of our voyage has begun! We are on our way to our first overnight stop, Kings Point, a town on the western edge of Long Island. The weather is foggy, but we have our course charted, and this will be a good test of our navigational skills. Ann is at the helm, and it's hard to believe we have actually left Centerport, Long Island, and are truly on our way to Florida.

I have to admit, as we were preparing to drop the mooring, I became somewhat tentative and said, "Maybe we should wait until tomorrow for a sunny day."

Ann shot me a look as she exclaimed, "Are you kidding?" I really wasn't, but I realized she was right. If we couldn't deal with a little fog, we had no business going at all. I am a sailor, so I guess it's time to act like one.

How fitting for my car to die yesterday, a sign perhaps—it's time to leave the land. John and Eileen, longtime friends of mine, visited and gave *Perpetual* and the crew a once-over with high marks. Eileen and I worked together as nurses years ago and became great friends. Captain John was the person who introduced me to sailing twenty-two years ago, and so his expertise is more than valuable. He now teaches at Kings Point Merchant Marine Academy and has invited us to tie up at their dock so we can be well-positioned to pass through the dreaded Hell Gate at slack tide. This is crucial as this tidal strait in New York's East River can have currents running up to five knots, and that's about our hull speed.

Our last evening in Centerport was marked by a visit from our wise older friends, Evie and Joan. Such a stretch for them both, nervously taking the launch boat and climbing aboard *Perpetual*. Evie brought us Holy water and various medals to keep us safe, which we fastened to the grab rails in the galley. They wound up staying for dinner as we all enjoyed barbecued chicken, corn, and potatoes. The wine was sour, which was probably a good thing, as our heads were clear, and concentrating on our compass course was easier.

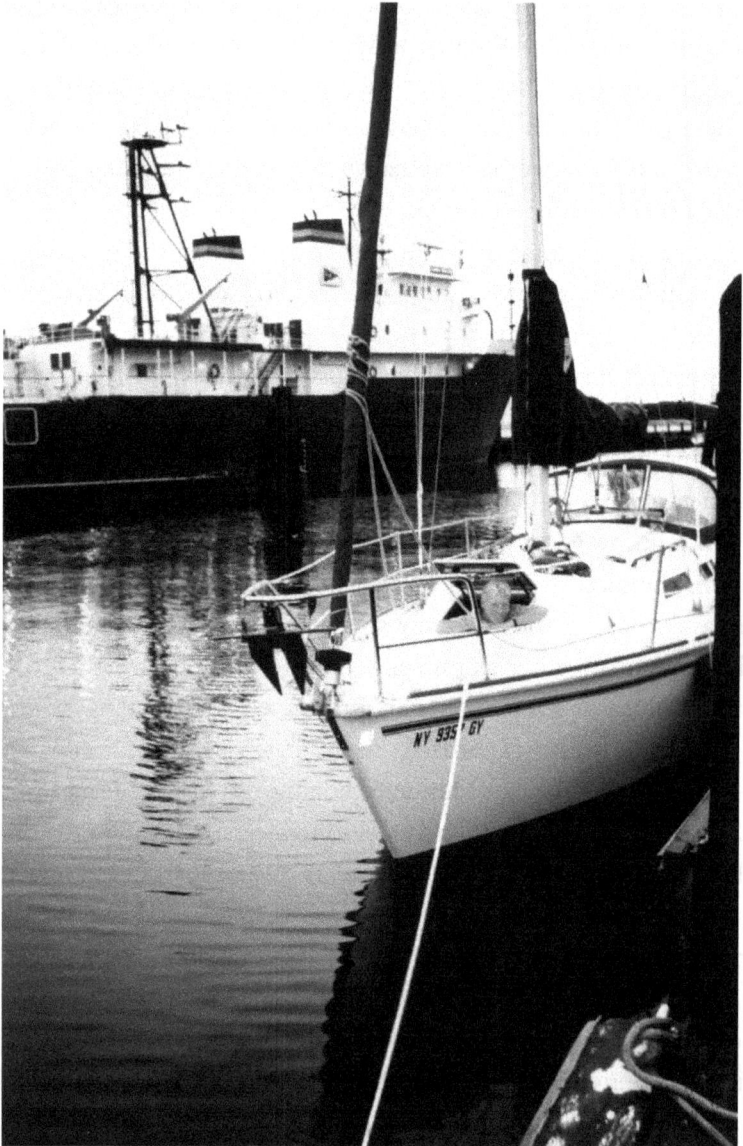

Perpetual across from the King's Pointer

When I reflect on the last few months of preparation, which included renting Ann's house, living from pillar to post, outfitting *Perpetual,* and helping with my daughter's beautiful wedding, these humble surroundings, now our home, are amazingly comfortable and peaceful. *Perpetual* does look beautiful. On the port side of the cabin are special photos of all our kids and friends. We have fresh flowers in the cockpit. Our fold-up bikes are neatly stored away in the starboard locker. We have block ice in the icebox, which should last a few days, enough food for at least a week, and all the other stuff has miraculously found a place.

We are on our way to Florida; only eleven hundred miles to go!

We arrived at Kings Point early in the afternoon as the skies opened up to torrential rain. Safely docked across from the *Kings Pointer,* the training ship for the merchant marine cadets, we donned our foul weather gear and headed to meet Captain John, who gave us a tour of this mammoth ship. It felt like the movie "Mr. Roberts" as we strolled the decks. Up on the bridge, he reviewed our route on the immense nautical charts. He printed our tides and currents on the computer. It was a real kick. He is such an incredible person. He had to make sure we had two bags of ice and the remnants of the chocolate chip cookies from his lunch with the cadets.

Lots of hugs, and he was off, back to Northport, and for us, it was time for a wee nap on *Perpetual*. How delightful this new life is.

Later, we took a stroll around the grounds of the school and found the setting quite beautiful. Ann's Uncle Frank attended Kings Point in the 40s, so we snapped some photos that we could show him if and when we make it to New Bern, North Carolina, where he lives.

We had to turn on our little TV as President Clinton addressed the Lewinsky situation and indeed admitted to an improper relationship with Monica Lewinsky. Oh my!

We feasted on our left over chicken, corn, and potatoes and those delicious chocolate chip cookies for dessert. It was magical, with the lights of New York's Throgs Neck Bridge just a few thousand feet away. Tomorrow will be *Perpetual's* debut through the East River.

NEW YORK HARBOR AND
THE MIGHTY ATLANTIC OCEAN

August 18, 1998

We awoke at 5 a.m., began our journey down NY harbor, and arrived at Hell Gate at 7:45 as planned, with no issues. Motoring down the East River was another story. Dodging the massive container ships kept us both keenly alert. Seeing my brother Tom at 53rd St, yelling "Bon voyage, Bon voyage" was quite a hoot. He told us he would be there, and he was. The sky was a magnificent blue, and the sun was beaming. Ann and I kissed under every bridge. The magnificent Twin Towers stood tall as we went under my favorite bridge, the Brooklyn Bridge. We put our sails up just before going under the Verrazano Bridge and sailed to Sandy Hook at 5 knots.

After anchoring the boat, we showered in the cockpit. The weather was looking rather ominous, with reports of thunderstorms in Long Island, but the anchor was holding well, and that was crucial.

We were quite tired from the excitement of the day and turned in early. Not much of a restful night with the wind blowing out of the northeast, and not much protection.

August 19, 1998

We contemplated not leaving. Weather station predictions of five to seven feet seas in the ocean with winds up to 20 knots. We decided to put a reef in the mainsail, which would reduce the sail and hopefully make the ride smoother, and pulled up the anchor, which was pretty dug in, but we couldn't complain as it held us. We got started around ten and rounded the hook with waves coming in all directions. We had life jackets on, fastened our harnesses, and momentarily thought about turning back but decided to forge ahead as the seas finally gave up the erratic chop once we got further south. We were now in the mighty Atlantic Ocean, and It demanded our full attention.

It was quite a welcome sight to spot the Manasquan Inlet in New Jersey, which we navigated rather easily, and found the Brielle Marine Basin, where we docked *Perpetual* for the night. Rich, Ann's brother, and his wife Marlene met us, and off we went to a pleasant restaurant in Spring Lake, a beautiful seaside town. We could barely keep our eyes open as Rich gave us some instructions on our newly acquired laptop computer.

So happy to be back in our v-berth where sleep finally won out in spite of the train bridge only a few yards away.

August 20, 1998

It was an incredible day for our sail to Atlantic City, New Jersey. The wind was blowing eight knots, and we were motor sailing with the waves at our port stern, which gave us some speed. However, it also managed to push us too close to shore, and we inadvertently hit a shoal right off Egg Harbor. It was somewhat hairy, but we were free again in a matter of seconds, and we hurriedly changed course and headed out towards England. "Going aground in the ocean seems like poor form," as Ann so aptly stated in her southern drawl, and finally, we were laughing.

Finding the Atlantic City inlet from the north is a bit tricky, and we were still a bit traumatized by our brush with the ocean's bottom; however, we made it safely, never to find buoy 17, which, according to the Waterway Guide is where one could anchor and that had been the plan. Instead, we were going under a bridge with a sixty-foot clearance, and by the way, we were not altogether certain about the height of our mast. Prayers were said as we went through and held our breath.

It was especially relieving to find Harrah's marina and casino. It was not that we were gamblers, but we could finally stop and take a deep breath. As a bonus, the most exquisite sunset appeared.

August 21-23, 1998

So much has happened since my last entry. Our sail from Atlantic City to Cape May seemed longer than we thought. We had fierce head winds and could only motor. The Inlet was a bit tricky, but finally, the chop gave way to slack water, and we breathed a sigh of relief. We had planned to anchor, but since we needed fuel, we headed for a marina and quickly decided to stay put. We were pretty beat but exhilarated with the ocean part of our journey now behind us. It was "Miller time," so we split a Corona and toasted to life.

We decided to stay in Cape May for a couple of days. So, on Saturday, we got our bikes out of the locker and went for an exploratory ride.

Cape May is a beautiful seaside town with lovely Victorian Inns dotting the coastline. It was a hot summer's day, but the cool breeze while riding our bikes was delightful. What a treat to find a park bench in the shade, where we could write postcards, basically stare into space, and enjoy people-watching.

We are not crazy about marina living and much prefer being at a mooring or anchoring, so we checked out the anchorage near the Coast Guard station. However, with laundry to be done and Marie and Carol arriving on Sunday, we decided to stay put.

Just heard that a hurricane may be approaching the Northeast. Oh dear!

We had a delightful day with Marie, whom I've known since I was fifteen, and Carol, her partner. We picnicked on the beautiful lighthouse grounds, feasting on shrimp cocktail, potato, and chicken salad. We would be passing the lighthouse again tomorrow as we would sail through the Cape May Canal.

We plan to leave tomorrow, and the weather report sounds favorable. Incidentally, we managed to ascertain the height of the mast. Forty-five feet is the magic number, as we have quite a few bridges to contend with as we continue on this magnificent journey.

As we started to plot our course for the next day, my trusty navigator wanted to go up the Cohansey River, which is still in New Jersey and seemed to be the only place to stop before entering the Chesapeake and Delaware Canal. The Waterway Guide described it as "picturesque and charming," but we heard from a fellow boater that the current is too stiff for sailboats. That gave me some pause for concern. However, not to be deterred, Ann decided to call the marina and found out that a sailboat would have no problem as long as we timed the current correctly.

That evening, Ann plotted the course on the chart so we could readily find the buoys.

August 24, 1998

On Monday morning, we left Cape May. Leaving the slip became quite frenetic and without any finesse, to say the least. I hope we can get better at this. I have to admit, it was never my forte, and I tried to do it too quickly without talking it through. It was a lesson, hopefully learned.

The trip down the Cape May Canal was quick, and before we knew it, we were in the Delaware River, which was quite choppy. The visibility was not great, but we decided to hoist up the sails and follow the

Annie Feeney

compass in search of the plotted buoys, leaving land out of sight. We did not want to get into the shipping lanes as those "moving apartment buildings," as I refer to those monstrous container ships, can come barreling down very quickly. It's terrifying to look behind and out of the haze, see these gigantic monsters approaching, and realize we are the burdened vessel.

It was truly a welcome sight to spot the Ship John Shoal lighthouse that was two miles from the entrance to the Cohansey River. The tide was indeed in our favor as we entered and continued up this three-mile, hairpin passageway. The marina that we planned to go to had no room, so we opted for the working boatyard further up the river. As we approached the dock, the current was fierce, and it was a miracle that we did not hit the oyster boat in front of us, even with reverse in full throttle.

The boatyard proprietor was not very friendly and started to bad mouth "women" and "God-damn teachers who think they know boating because they read some books and then wind up crashing into my pilings." Well, here we were, women and one of us, a teacher. A professor, I might add. Thankfully, we didn't hit anything, but his rude attitude scared us both, and Ann wanted to leave the dock and anchor. I, on the other hand, was concerned that the current would create problems with anchoring. Since we needed ice and "Mr. RedNeck" had none, we decided to dig out our bikes and ride to town.

It was just what we needed as we rode past beautiful farmlands and quaint homes. The bikes were such a blessing to have. We would never have been able to walk and keep the ice from melting, and even in this scorching heat, the cool breeze, created by riding, was so refreshing.

Back at the boatyard, the oyster boat owner, "the Goddamn drunk," as Mr. Redneck described him, had returned. He and another guy were revving up the engine, and it looked like they were leaving. However, that was not the case. At this point, Ann was quite adamant about anchoring out, and I, too, was beginning to have some doubts about staying at the dock. As Ann began to pack up the bikes, the two men came over looking for a cigarette and commented, "Wow, check out these fancy expensive bikes." They both sounded slightly inebriated, and there was no one around except us and these two guys. Ann quickly answered "They are neither fancy nor expensive, and sorry, we don't smoke."

Down below, we both began to feel very vulnerable and weighed our options of anchoring, but we quickly realized it was better to remain at the dock in case we had to call the police. We did not have a gun, but we did have a sharp knife and some heavy winch handles, which we laid out on the cockpit steps. It felt like a Stephen King novel, and we were the leading ladies. Yikes!! Both of us were very edgy, to say the least, peeking out of the cabin ports every few minutes. Finally, they pulled away in a car as we breathed a sigh of relief and decided to fix dinner.

An hour later, they returned but, to our amazement, boarded their boat and left the dock. "Oh God, thank you!" And this is just the beginning of our trip. It was time to shift the space and leave our scary thoughts behind, so we ate dinner and crawled into our v-berth with the hopes and prayers that there would be no unexpected visitors again.

We slept like logs, exhausted from the fright, and awoke early so we could get underway quickly. The morning sky was magical as Ann kept repeating, "Take this in right now, it's wonderful." And how right she was because, in one moment, that bliss can change, and so it did. Coming out of the Cohancy Inlet, we were taking care to stay in the deepest part of the channel by keeping the boat's starboard (i.e., right) side inside of the green buoy we were approaching. Nevertheless, we were met with a grinding thud as our keel dug into the ground, causing the boat to stop abruptly. Although the sound was sickening, and we seemed to be stuck for an eternity, it was only a matter of minutes before we were able to steer ourselves free. It took a while for both of us to get over the fear of "doing that again" as we nervously watched the depth-sounder and threaded our way through the shoals and out into the deep, wide channel of the Delaware River.

We spent the next couple of hours mulling over the next new experience we were facing: negotiating the Chesapeake & Delaware Canal. In our minds, we pictured the canal as a narrow, crowded waterway, and we grew more and more anxious looking at the size and speed of most of the other vessels with which we were sharing the route. We arrived at the entrance to the canal about an hour before the tide changed and took some comfort in knowing that entering the unfamiliar waters in slack water would be in our favor. Four monstrous container ships appeared to be waiting out the tide as well, and we gladly decided to let them go first. After an hour had passed, and none of the container ships appeared to be moving, I took out my trusty binoculars and spotted a small sailboat entering the canal. Well, I thought, if she's venturing forward, not worrying about the huge monsters, we can just follow, and so we did, under the many bridges with nobody at our stern. Much of our fear dissipated as we saw the enormous width of the canal, which we later learned is 450 ft. I still experienced a momentary feeling of pure fear the first time I saw a huge container ship coming toward us and instinctively tried to hug the side of the canal. The feeling quickly passed, however, as did the ship, without incident—thank God—along with the realization that facing fear was becoming a central part of this new life.

We arrived at our intended destination, an anchor basin in Chesapeake City, and it was a very welcome sight. The anchor basin is just off this scenic marina and literally is a basin that just ends. According to the charts, ten feet of water prevails, so we set anchor and within a short time realized it was dragging-ugh! We then spotted a dock, but it had a no trespassing sign, so two very exhausted, cranky sailors tried anchoring again two more times and finally succeeded.

August 29, 1998

It's an amazing Saturday evening, and we're still in Chesapeake City. With all the talk of hurricane Bonnie, we decided this was the safest place to be, and it's quite beautiful sitting in the cockpit safe at anchor and viewing our scenic surroundings.

Earlier today, we managed to inflate and launch the dinghy, attach the engine, and ferry our bikes into town for a ride. It was not an easy task to attach the engine to the dinghy, and it was not without some differences of opinion on the safest way to do it. We are now watching this fellow sailor step into his dinghy and attach the engine single-handedly with such finesse. Put that on the list for mastering.

We have so enjoyed our stay here, enjoying exquisite cockpit showers and candlelit cockpit dinners with music echoing from the Chesapeake Inn as our anchor held, and our appreciation of this magical life and its blessings continue to unfold.

We are leaving here in the morning out into the Chesapeake Bay and heading up the Sassafras River to Maryland.

THE CHESAPEAKE BAY AND
ITS CAPTIVATING WONDERS

September 1, 1998

We are currently motor sailing on the Chesapeake. Ann is at the helm, methodically following the buoys as it can become very shallow quickly.

Our two-day stay in Georgetown was delightful as we picked up a mooring and had the luxury of hailing a launch that promptly would deliver us to land. There, we had complimentary use of bikes, which we used to stock up on much-needed groceries. The pool, however, was the highlight as the weather was incredibly hot. The evenings were cooler, and we enjoyed returning to *Perpetual* and making a simple dinner.

Living on a boat has a rhythm all of its own, and presently, we are loving this life.

September 2, 1998

We are currently going up the Chester River, which is a major tributary of the Chesapeake. Our destination is Chestertown, Maryland.

Our stay in Rock Hall was short but sweet. The marina is owned by a couple who come from Westchester, New York. That's where Ann and I currently live. It's a small world.

We almost got swamped by a tugboat wake and battled thousands of flies on our way, and it was a good thing we had a fly swatter, so the first order, when dockside, was to clean the boat in spite of our fatigue. We rewarded ourselves with a glorious swim in the pool and a marina shower, and we decided to visit the town in the morning. It was an early dinner, and it felt so good to tuck ourselves into our cozy v-berth. In spite of the rain periodically spraying our faces through the open hatch, we slept like logs. Woke up to rain and thunder and thought perhaps we would be staying another day, but Ann proclaimed, "Rain before seven, gone by eleven." Having never heard that before, I had my doubts as we walked to the America's Cup Cafe for breakfast. Lo and behold, upon leaving, there was the sun piercing through the clouds, and it was 10 a.m. Off to Chestertown.

September 4, 1998

We've been in Chestertown for two days enjoying this quaint historic gem, established in 1742. Many of the older homes still retain the flavor of a bygone era.

It was a long day getting here, and we were pretty weary and anxious about where to anchor because of the "cable area" marked on the chart. Not sure what that meant, but it gave us some concern. Finally, a local fisherman came by in his skiff and told us to throw the hook off the main channel, which we did, and it held.

My hay fever had been acting up, so en route, I decided to take an antihistamine, which almost did me in. We managed to get the dinghy pumped up and the engine on the dinghy and made our way into town, found a quiet little park, and ate our prepared lunch. I could barely stay awake, and Ann wanted to visit Washington College, so I gave in, with the idea that we could park at the library so I could sleep and she could write. The plan worked as I had a great sleep, returned to my normal self, and vowed never to take an antihistamine when it's daylight.

Back on *Perpetual*, we dined in the cockpit, watching a breathtaking sunset.

September 6, 1998

Today, we ventured into town with our bikes after we retrieved them from the locker, placed them in a sail bag, and carefully lowered them into the dinghy, thankfully without incident. It was a beautiful day for a bike ride, and we stopped for lunch at The Old Wharf Inn, where I had my first taste of Maryland crabcakes, and they were quite exquisite. I sometimes want to pinch myself—can't believe that we are experiencing all these amazing wonders.

Off to St Michaels, Maryland, in the morning, which, according to our Waterway Guide, is a must-visit with its manicured parks and great restaurants.

September 8, 1998

I can never keep up with my journal writing.

Anyway, it's a brisk Tuesday afternoon, and we are sitting at St Michael's Harbor Marina. We are supposed to be leaving, but our depth sounder is reading only four feet, which translates to five, and since our draft is almost five, we'll wait for the tide to come in. The place is so quiet. Everyone has returned home after Labor Day, and it's quite wonderful. The town had been so packed for the weekend, and this was a welcome change.

On our first night, we anchored about three miles outside the town in a place called Shaw Bay. Lots of boats, mostly sail, but plenty of room, where at night, it became purely magical with everyone's anchor lights aglow and the twinkling stars above. On Sunday morning, we motored to town. The harbor was packed with boats, but we found an anchorage just off the town dock and managed to maneuver our dinghy quickly into a vacant spot at the dock. The famous Crab Claw Restaurant was bursting with people, so we happily strolled around this quaint, scenic town and treated ourselves to lunch at the Town Dock Restaurant—my first ever Oysters Rockefeller, "Oh so good." We are having so much fun!

On Labor Day, we pulled into the marina and watched the parade of boats leave the harbor. We had made the right choice, anchoring out until the crowds died down. Our main events for the day were getting a pump out, washing the boat, and doing the laundry. Having completed it all, we rewarded ourselves with a refreshing swim in the pool, as the temperature was well over ninety degrees. Shopping would wait till the morning.

It feels a bit weird to think we are not returning to work, especially now that summer is officially over, but the truth is, we never feel bored. There is always something to do or something waiting to be done.

Like this morning, for instance, unpacking the bikes so we could do grocery shopping and transporting them onto the dock. Then there is locating where the store is, doing the shopping, and securing groceries onto the bikes; of course, that always includes ice, which provides its own challenge. Just having food, clean clothes, and sweet-smelling sheets can create such a feeling of well-being. I guess we take things for granted, living on land with all its conveniences, but here, our lives have become simpler and more direct in some ways. It's back to basics.

The dockmaster just informed us that since the water is still a bit shallow, we can stay another night "on the house" and leave with the morning tide. Even when all is good, it just got even better. It's time to play Scrabble!

September 11, 1998

Well, one thing you can be certain of, is that the weather can change in an instant, and honoring mother nature is a must. We are leaving St Michaels for the second time. Today, there are beautiful skies, and the water looks like glass.

It was quite a different story two mornings ago. We awoke early on September 9 and put a reef in the main because the weather station was calling for wind gusts of 30 knots. The wind was pretty stiff at the dock, and there was a considerable chop on the river. Out we ventured, and within twenty minutes, we knew that this had not been a wise decision. The gusts were up to 29, and we were heading right into the chop that was rather steep. I was at the helm, steering the boat and trying to maintain the course, but I was having difficulty holding the wheel steady enough to do so. We decided to return to St Michaels.

Reversing the course became tricky. We already had our life jackets on as we turned into the wind, which slowed us down and finally enabled us to reverse course. We literally surfed back into the harbor. Even though we landed on a sandbar while trying to anchor, we recovered quickly and felt amazingly relieved and thankful for our safe return. It was only 9 a.m., and people were most likely sleeping but perhaps now rudely awakened by the noisy newcomers.

Ann read, and I just stared into space for hours, interrupted only by napping. I felt beaten down and had fleeting thoughts of selling the boat and renting a condo. Ann could tell I was feeling defeated, and as we talked it through, it helped me conclude that we made the right decision in the long run by returning, and that's what is most important.

The next day, the wind was pretty gusty, so two smart sailors made the decision to remain another day.

Presently, we are sailing with only five knots of wind. Ann is at the helm, exclaiming how perfect it is. *Perpetual* is gliding through the water ever so steadily with just a faint sound of "swish," and the fleeting thought of abandoning ship for a condo has suddenly disappeared.

We made a split-second decision to go through the Knapps Narrows, which is the shortest route between the Eastern Bay and the Choptank River, our destination being Oxford, Maryland. Even though we hit depths of only 4.5 ft, we escaped any keel scraping.

It is the best of times and sometimes the worst of times, but the one thing that is constant is that it's always changing, and changing we must, in order to not only survive but to truly live.

We arrived in Oxford and anchored off a beach called the Strand. Our Waterway Guide is our Bible, as it gives us all the local info to find such peaceful places. We love the seclusion of anchoring especially when it's holding well. There were only three other boats, and we observed how our neighbors had managed to cover their lifelines with sheets and "voila, the Oxford shower curtain," as we named it. How clever! We immediately made our own and experienced glorious hot showers in the cockpit, thanks to our sun shower, which had been heating up for days.

The next day, we decided to explore Oxford. A few chores first: motor and bikes carefully lowered to the dinghy, attaching the motor to the transom, and then the trek to the beach, all carefully maneuvered.

All went as planned, and we were excitedly exploring one of the most beautiful towns in Maryland, with its attractive, meticulously cared-for homes lining the streets and almost all with views of the Trent Avon River. We ate lunch at Pier Street Restaurant, and I sampled soft shell crabs for the first time, but they were not my favorite. I guess you have to acquire a taste for this delicacy. We decided to leave our bikes in town overnight since we would be back again the next day. As we were locking them, a passer-by exclaimed, "You don't have to do that, no crime here." Our New York mentality lingers.

September 13, 1998

Another glorious day, and we're off to the tennis courts for some much-needed exercise. We worked up a pretty good sweat, but that did not stop us from going to an awesome brunch at Schooner Landing, an "all you can eat" buffet, so of course, we had to sample everything, including eggs benedict, shrimp, crab legs, pancakes, pasta and of course scrumptious pastries, enjoying every morsel. Good thing we don't have access to this very often; however, we have to tell our friends and family back in NY about this place. Perhaps a Fall weekend next year? It only took us five weeks to get here by boat, which probably translates to eight hours by car.

September 14, 1998

Left Oxford and headed for Solomons Island, Maryland, which would be a stopover before going to Smith Island. The forecast called for 10 knots, which would make a great sail to cross the Chesapeake, so we thought. Instead, we encountered heavy head winds and seas and motored most of the eight and a half hours—not a comfortable day.

We came into a pretty shoddy marina with an equally shabby washing machine. Instructions read: to hold the lid open with a stick. Enough said, we got the wash done and crawled into the v-berth for some much-needed sleep.

September 16, 1998

Smith Island was a must-stop for us, having read about it in a book called "Secluded Islands of the Atlantic Coast." The author, David Yeadon, had a special fondness as he describes "loving the winding lanes, its oyster shell tracks leading off into hammocks of eucalyptus and pine lining the shady main street dotted with white victorian cottages." This remains to be seen, as we have not ventured off the boat and are currently enjoying our morning coffee.

Our sail here was rather rough as we pounded into four-foot waves soaking the v-berth. Must remember to close the hatch when underway. Sights of land disappeared for most of the day. We literally saw no boats for hours, and then out of the haze, there would be one of those formidable "moving apartment buildings" that would immediately demand action.

Entering the harbor was quite a task and completely successful, we were not. The chart showed depths of six feet, but even with lining up the buoys, we managed to find three feet. We went aground twice and managed to get off easily the first time, but the second time, we were on the inside of the dock and pretty dug in.

Two guys on the dock called out, "Ladies, you're on the wrong side of the dock." After fastening a line to the cleat, they pulled *Perpetual* free. We then found the correct side and pulled up where a hand written sign said, "Overnight Docking $15 Daily - Pay at Rukes, Red Store on right." We thanked our helpers, who promptly left. Well, at least the price is right, but for now, it was Miller Time, and we shared a Coors Light, cautiously, I might add. This is supposed to be a dry island, having been converted to strict Methodism after the first settlers developed a reputation for "lawlessness and drunken behavior," as our book describes.

It wasn't until later that evening that I wondered about the so-called dryness of the island as the guy who pulled us off the shoal came sauntering down the dock, inviting us for a drink at the Ewell Tide Inn. Again, I thanked him for his help and expressed how tired we were. At first, he became insistent and then finally backed off. We began to experience deja vu of our incident on the Cohansey River. Ann decided we needed a weapon, so we placed the winch handle on the chart table.

This part of cruising doesn't thrill us. Two women alone on a sailboat is very rare, and here we were, tethered to a rickety dock on a remote island in the middle of the Chesapeake Bay and feeling a tad bit vulnerable, to say the least.

Back on Smith Island, there was much to be explored. We were docked at Ruke's dock, and having paid for two nights, we were now being told that a big sightseeing boat was arriving and it would need the dock. Mr Ruke was quite apologetic, however, and found us another spot to tie up. So off to the Driftwood Grocery Store, "just a piece up the river."

We were met by Steve, the owner, who immediately welcomed us and exclaimed, "If anyone gives you trouble, let me know." That felt rather comforting, I must say.

The store had minimal supplies but certainly enough for our needs. The whole Island, though, depended on it. Across the street was the post office, and the whole scene was something from another era.

Striking up a conversation with some of the islanders was easy, and listening to their stories was fascinating. Those who lived their whole life on this island were very content with their way of life. Crabbing was their main focus, and you could see the dilapidated piers where the crab shells are shed to produce soft-shell crabs.

One eighty-four-year-old gent told me he just had open heart surgery in Baltimore and then went to "one of those rehab places, couldn't understand why that was necessary." He looked great and said he felt just fine. Thinking to myself, perhaps it was because you went to the rehab place. Having been part of setting up a brand new subacute and rehab unit in Westchester, New York, last year, I know first hand the value of such units.

We biked the island and followed the blue bus which we had read about. It was full of senior tourists and would lead us to the famous Bayside Inn.

There, we found an all-you-can-eat buffet for $10.95. Crab balls, clam fritters, corn pudding, crab bisque, ham, and salads were just a few of the choices, and all outstanding. And the desserts, oh my! It was quite amazing to watch all the tourists pouring in by boat and bus, and by four, all was quiet again. The restaurant and gift store closed for the day, and life on this small island returned to its tranquil state.

Two sailboats pulled into Ruke's dock, and we met Sherrie and Mike on their Pearson 39 and Sue and Kurt on their Saber 39, very congenial folks on vacation from New Jersey. We exchanged some sailing stories and planned to see each other tomorrow on Tangier Island.

September 17, 1998

We left the dock around eleven so we could have high tide in our favor. Today would be a short sail, and we were able to hoist sails with a gentle breeze guiding us. I was having a miserable hay fever attack by then and was absolutely no help to Ann as I sneezed at least a hundred times. Being mindful of the channel buoys became our focus in between my "achoos." Alas, we were safely docked at the marina and met by the owners, who welcomed us. Sherrie and Mike were docked alongside.

Tangier Island seemed grander than Smith and actually has double the population. As we began exploring the island, hoping to find a pharmacy, we came upon a clinic that, to our amazement, was open.

The staff flies in once a week from Whitestone, Virginia. The waiting room was filled with the local islanders, and everyone seemed to know one another. The physician was great and gave me a prescription for Allegra and some samples that would last a couple of weeks. He told me how rewarding his weekly visits were, as the people were so appreciative. He even had an opening for a Nurse Practitioner. Wow, that's food for thought.

I quickly swallowed a pill and knew relief was on the way.

Mike and Sherrie had mentioned that if we wanted to sample the cooking at Crocket's Chesapeake Inn, we would have to be there at around five. After a luxurious shower, we found Crocket's and feasted at long tables, with interesting conversation flowing while we ate great comfort food. Afterward, it was time to take a long walking tour of Tangiers and hopefully burn off some calories.

September 18, 1998

Today looked a bit ominous, and the forecast was for possible thunderstorms. I was content to make meatballs down below in our cabin as Ann went topside to wash down the boat and talk about "weather" with our fellow dock mates. I felt perfectly happy listening to music from "The King and I" as the aroma of tomato sauce permeated the cabin. I hadn't noticed the sun now shining as Ann came down below, announcing, "Everyone is leaving, and there is only a minimal chance of a storm." I was not thrilled, but I conceded and prepared for the journey across the Chesapeake to Deltaville, Virginia.

The weather remained good and even permitted hoisting sails, which helped my mood. However, as we neared the end of the trip, my navigator became very concerned about the shoaling in the harbor. Suffice it to say once doubt and fear come aboard, differing opinions often occur. The good news, though, is that we both gave in and focused on the present situation and managed to find our way safely to the dock, and this time it was the correct side.

September 19, 1998

Woke up to beautiful sunshine and decided to bike to the supermarket which was a good three miles away. It was delightful to return with lots of groceries and have a cool swimming pool awaiting us.

What could be better than having a candlelight dinner under the stars? Of course, my Tangier Island meatballs were quite a success, too.

I'm sure there are folks who would ask how two women could live on a small sailboat for weeks and still enjoy it. It definitely has its ups and downs, but on a night like this, it's purely magical. I rest my case.

September 20, 1998

We awoke early in anticipation of a long day's sail, our destination being the York River. We are making our way south down the Chesapeake and need to take advantage of the good weather since Ann's family has planned a family reunion in New Bern, North Carolina, on Columbus Day weekend.

Listening to our TV weather forecast reporting one hurricane after another is sort of unnerving. Bonnie seems so long ago, and already they're talking about Karl. Puerto Rico has been pretty devastated by George, and now there's talk about evacuating the Florida Keys. It clearly keeps us focused.

Back on the water, the wind was very light coming from the north, so we basically motored. We found the York River and began following the channel buoys. The only problem was they didn't match what we saw on the chart. Here we go again with some momentary chaos! It wasn't until we saw another sailboat on the same course asking a local waterman if he was in the channel and got the ok, that we began to settle down. A few miles later, we found Sarah Creek, a beautiful anchorage off a marina which the Waterway Guide described as charging a small fee for the use of amenities. What could be better than that?

September 21, 1998

Since we are in the thick of history, with Williamsburg only eleven miles away, we decided to rent a car and stay overnight in a hotel. We would leave *Perpetual* at anchor, a first in thirty-four days. We were very excited to become true tourists for twenty-four hours. Ann was particularly happy that she could watch the Clinton Grand Jury Deposition on television.

After doing laundry and taking a $2 shower, we were off to colonial Williamsburg to have what Ann coined a "Cinderella overnight." We were like two giddy teenagers.

We found a perfectly pleasant hotel three blocks from historic downtown. We even found a CVS where I filled my hay fever prescription for $2.50 instead of $60 if my plan hadn't been accepted.

What a treat to take a hotel shower and watch the news while we sip a gin and tonic.

The village was such fun, with people dressed in colonial garb and beautiful period homes lining the streets. We had a truly romantic dinner at Shields Tavern in a completely candlelit parlor. Singers in traditional dress, with guitars and mandolins, serenaded "the women sailors from NY." Yes, it was indeed a Cinderella Night!

The next morning, we still had some time, so we found another quaint tavern and enjoyed a splendid lunch of Welsh rarebit and turkey. Then, it was back to Sara Creek, where *Perpetual* awaited our arrival, safe and sound.

The next morning was quite windy, and our plan was to head for Norfolk, Virginia. However, after listening to the weather announcing winds of 30 knots and five-foot seas, we wisely decided to stay put. Instead, we would take a dinghy ride to find the shopping center that the Waterway Guide described was "at the end of the creek in a marsh grass-lined drainage canal."

Lewis and Clark, as I named us, almost turned back, especially when we were in the thick of the marsh and heard a snake-like sound. We were literally at the end of the creek and could see the stores but couldn't find a path to access them. Finally, we found the drainage canal, tied the dinghy to a tree branch, and located the path. Out of the marsh came Lewis and Clark, feeling very triumphant. We found a hair salon where I got a much-needed haircut, and Ann bought out the Dollar store. Armed with five bags of groceries, we carefully retraced our way through the muddy marsh, found our dinghy, and made the three-mile trek back to the marina dock for a brief stop at the marine store. Ann wanted to check a more recent chart regarding the York River's buoys. Upon return, our engine failed, but we had our oars, so Lewis and Clark rowed back to *Perpetual* without any problem. We will deal with the outboard engine another day.

September 24, 1998

We awoke early to prepare for our sail to Norfolk, Virginia. The weather looked great, and of course, we verified that with NOAA radio.

After a pumpout, which necessitated returning to the dock where we could empty our sewage waste and replenish our water supply, we were off.

Today would be tricky since we now knew that the buoys in the York River had been changed, but my brilliant Navigator had viewed a brand new chart in the marine store and plotted the correct markings for the York River.

The trip was rather uneventful until we hit Norfolk and Hampton Roads. Those massive container ships began to appear again as we left the Chesapeake Bay. There were barges and tugboats coming from all directions. The piers were lined with aircraft carriers and Navy destroy-ers. It was a thrilling sight. The wind was just right for a downwind sail as we unfurled the jib. It was definitely a moment of pure joy!

In the distance, we spotted a tugboat flashing bright lights. As we got closer, the tug veered off, and right next to *Perpetual*, a submarine emerged!! We were momentarily stunned and quickly realized that the tug's bright lights must have been an alert signal for our little sailboat to give way, which we hadn't. No time to think about that now, so I immediately started the engine and pulled in the jib just in case there would be more ahead. Oh my God!! Thankfully, there weren't, as we managed to find the Lafayette River, where we set anchor for the night and processed this unbelievable occurrence. Who was the burdened vessel, and who had the right of way?

ENTERING THE INTRACOASTAL WATERWAY AND THE GREAT DISMAL SWAMP

September 25, 1998

Today is the day to decide whether we would take the Dismal Swamp Canal route or the Virginia Cut. The canal sounded so picturesque, but there was a possibility that it could be closed because of falling depths. We would have to call the Corps of Engineers.

As we left the anchorage and headed toward the Elizabeth River, we noticed two other sailboats behind us that quickly passed by, and that was totally fine. It's nice to have company as we begin to contend with bascule bridges, similar to draw bridges, and have to be called for openings. Today, we'll have six. In the lead boat, a fellow sailor we met this morning from New Orleans is traveling solo and has made this trip four times. It's hard for me to think that anyone would want to go on this trip alone, but he seemed perfectly content.

We were approaching our first bridge with bells ringing, traffic stopping, and the bridge opening as three sailboats glided through. It was absolutely thrilling. Oh, I forgot to mention we entered the Intracoastal Waterway today, also known as the ICW or the ditch, mile 0 at Red Buoy 36, opposite the Portsmouth Naval Hospital. We will now be following some different markers along with the red and green buoys. The yellow triangle is kept to starboard, the right side and the yellow square or rectangle is kept to port, the left.

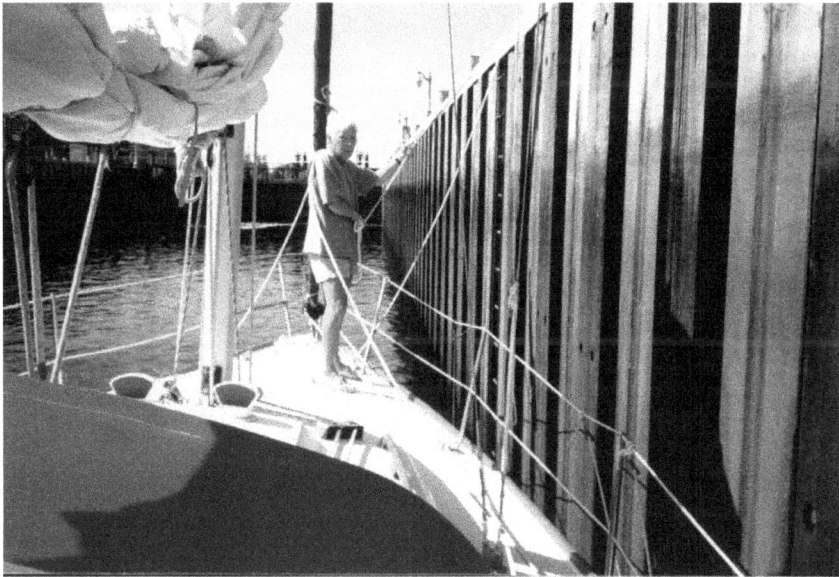

We found out that the Dismal Swamp was open and turned to starboard with no other boats in sight, a somewhat eerie feeling but nevertheless exciting. *Perpetual* entered the quiet, dark waters of the oldest man-made waterway in the country. Our hope was to make the lock by 11. We saw ahead what seemed to be a dead end when, all of a sudden, it opened, and we put the diesel into full throttle. As we entered, the lock tender was shouting, "Throw me your lines," after chastising us for being late (five minutes). Thank goodness we already had our fenders to starboard as our trusty Waterway Guide had instructed, and now we were locked into the lock where water would pour in to elevate us eight feet; all we had to do was hold on to the bow and stern lines that had been secured to the dock way above us. It sounded simple enough in theory, but then my navigator looked at me and said, "I'm terrified!" It was then I yelled to the lock tender, "We are new to this, and I would appreciate you knowing that." That said, it was time to "let go," not the lines but the fear, as the water started gushing in and *Perpetual* was raised eight feet higher. In a matter of twenty minutes, all was done, and the gates opened, and we were free to go.

The Dismal Swamp

The lock tender then had to jump in his truck and drive to open up the drawbridge for us. A great deal of work for one boat. As we waved goodbye, we thanked him profusely for his patience and clear instructions. He then asked where we were heading, and we answered, "Florida, and we'll be returning in the summer."

"Well then, if you ever get there, bring me back a conch shell," and so, we will.

He then instructed us on the importance of proceeding slowly through the canal as Hurricane Bonnie had caused a lot of debris, including tree branches that could be submerged. We were now traveling at a snail's pace through the drawbridge that he was tending when all of a sudden, fire engine sirens were blaring, and he was yelling to us, "Move faster." It took a minute to register that opening the bridge was now preventing the fire truck from getting through. I immediately pushed the throttle forward, causing a wake for a docked trawler on the other side who reprimanded me for now going too fast but then, in a much friendlier tone, "By the way, we met you in St Michaels." As we passed him, I remembered we had indeed met him and his partner, but for now, I was just thankful that the whole "lock" ordeal was over and we were now in the tranquil surroundings of the Great Dismal Swamp where we could take some slow deep breaths.

It genuinely was a very different experience, surrounded by lush Cypress trees on each side of the canal. It felt like we were moving through a path in a forest. The width being only forty feet in some spots. The water was brown because of the tannic acid from the trees. (the lock tender had related that piece of info to us). The sunlight actually laid a path on the water, which looked like a mirror reflecting the trees. Route 17 ran parallel with passing cars, the only reminder of civilization around. We were alone in the splendor and tranquility of this not-so-dismal body of water.

We almost missed the Visitors Center of North Carolina, where we would be stopping for the night since we were now using a book Jordan, Ann's son, had given us that measured everything in statute miles, and we were still using nautical miles. There were two boats tied up at the dock as we were passing, so I yelled back, "Is this the Visitors Center?" and the answer was "Yes." So, having passed the dock, it was with great concentration that *Perpetual* would be turned around in this narrow space. It was not our calmest docking maneuver, but within minutes, our lines were secured with the help of fellow boaters, and we were now safely docked in North Carolina.

Our new neighbors were sailors from Maine, and each of the two boats had two elderly couples and one grandchild. They were all in great shape and had recently retired to Harrington, Maine. One of the women was on the Health Board, and when she heard I was a Gerontological Nurse Practitioner, she asked if I would consider moving as their elderly population was growing, and that's what was needed.

Anyway, what lovely people! We all shared various sailing adventures just standing on the dock in North Carolina like we knew each other forever.

September 26, 1998

Up nice and early to complete our trek on the Dismal. We bid farewell to our boat buds with a "Maybe we'll see you in Maine."

It was a beautiful sunny day, and we marveled again at how the sun laid a magnificent path through this not-at-all dismal body of water, bordered by abundant vegetation and wildlife.

As we entered the South Mills lock, we now felt confident. We would be lowered eight feet, and we felt like "old hands." Fear of the unknown had now become known as we handed our lines to the dockmaster with an air of confidence and proceeded to descend and then be released into the Pasquotank River.

We were now on our way to Elizabeth City and excited to meet the famous "Rose Buddies," who, according to our Waterway Guide, would welcome incoming boaters, offering free dock space and host a wine and cheese party at the harbor when at least five transient boats were present. Two men, Fred Fearing and Joe Kramer, started the group in 1980, and it got its name from their signature presentation of roses to visiting crews. In 1983, due primarily to the Rose Buddies, Elizabeth City was named the City of Hospitality.

We were a bit disappointed that upon our somewhat early arrival in the harbor, we were met by no welcoming Rose Buddies and saw no other transient boats. But, a couple of hours later, we spotted a nice-looking elderly man traveling down the dock in a golf cart, who introduced himself as Fred Fearing and, pointing to some nearby rose bushes, handed Ann a pair of shears to "cut two roses for two lovely ladies." As we were making our acquaintances, a trawler was approaching the dock, and to our surprise, it was Bob and Colleen, the couple we first met in St. Michaels, Md., and again in the Dismal Swamp. We quickly helped them with their lines and introduced them to Fred, who promptly invited the crews of our two boats to a special wine and cheese party at his home, "six blocks up, the house with the almond tree in front."

It was a pleasant get-together as we gathered under the almond tree and listened to Fred tell one story after another. He had a captive audience, and it was hard for anyone else to get a word in edgewise, but on a balmy Saturday evening, as we sipped wine and listened, it was just fine.

September 27, 1998

We promised to get Bob the Sunday NY Times. Little did we know that one could buy a week-old Times for $3.50, so we did, not realizing that, of course, it was a week old. It wasn't until way into reading the news that it finally dawned on Ann. Bob and Colleen had a good laugh, especially after Ann tried to return the paper in a polite manner and was met with quite an attitude from the proprietor, who exclaimed, "You boaters think you're God." Oh well, lesson learned, read the date.

We spent most of the day on the boat reading and learning more about our diesel from Bob. Fred arrived on the dock to greet two new arrivals. Still not enough to host a party at the dock, but insisted on everyone coming to his house. It's very evident that Fred doesn't like no for an answer, so we lead the group off to the house with the almond tree. After an hour of listening to Fred's stories, we made our escape with Colleen and Bob and treated ourselves to a lovely dinner at the dock.

We have decided to stay another day since a cold front will be arriving tomorrow. Crossing the Albemarle Sound could be tricky since it is shallow, and the waves can be steep and unpredictable. A more pressing problem, though, was that Fred invited us for lunch tomorrow. We told him we were probably leaving in the morning but would let him know by 8 a.m. Oh dear!

September 28, 1998

Life in Elizabeth City could totally revolve around Fred and his stories, and since we weren't leaving today, it would have been hard to get out of our lunch date. In truth, we had laundry to do and needed to prepare for tomorrow's sail across the Albemarle Sound.

I didn't want to hurt his feelings, and Ann and I were going round and round about who should tell him. At the point the conversation was becoming ridiculous, I realized I needed to practice being more assertive. I hopped on my bike and rode to the house with the "almond tree in front," and my "Sorry we can't join you for lunch" was accepted, and that was it. All that angst I had brought on myself. I felt free and somewhat victorious as I rode back to the dock.

After doing our various chores, it was time to take a break and relax. There were quite a number of boats now docked, and oh my, here comes Fred on his cart hailing, "I need help with the party tonight, girls; I'll be back at five."

The party was great, and the newcomers mostly lived aboard big trawlers. Fred had a new audience and was in his glory, and for that, we were grateful. It was very enjoyable exchanging stories with the women, two of whom were quite surprised that we were doing this trip alone as neither of them ever took the helm. Their husbands were the "captains." Ann and I gently encouraged them to learn just in case their husbands got sick. One of the women then offered that her husband has had heart problems, and she is going to insist he start teaching her.

We all toasted to "women at the helm."

September 29, 1998

Woke early in anticipation of our rendezvous with the dreaded Albemarle. I was particularly unnerved having had a conversation with one of the trawler captains last eve when I asked if he was familiar with ranges, a new term I had come across in my Waterway Guide readings. His answer, in a very condescending tone, was, "You have no business going any further south if you don't know what a range is." I secretly wondered to myself, if I were a man, would he have answered that way, maybe? Anyway, I was left with feelings of doubt and shared them with Ann, who listened and said just what I wanted to hear: "We will figure it out, like we have so far." Indeed, we will, as my self-confidence was beginning to return.

As we headed out the river to the Albemarle Sound, the wind was kicking up, but the seas were relatively calm. Bob and Colleen were behind us for a short time and proceeded to take a different course that eventually would bring them and us to the same destination, the Alligator River Marina. We hoisted our sails and had the most beautiful sustained tack since leaving Long Island. The knot meter read 6.4 at times. We were both in our glory. The feared Albemarle was now our friend.

Bob radioed to warn us to be careful of the breakwater coming in as his depth sounder read four feet at times. We were spared the shoal and tied up to a clean but sparse marina. It was so nice to throw our lines at people we now know who invited us to watch a movie on their boat this evening. We were feeling pretty exhausted, but after a quick shower and something to eat, we regained some energy and climbed aboard *Long Shot,* a fairly large Trawler with all the amenities of home, including a galley with a fridge and microwave. This was luxury!

Bob had met some new arrivals, husband and wife, aboard a large sailboat, *Jambalaya,* and invited them to join us. Instead of watching a movie, we ended up talking over some wine and popcorn. He was a cardiologist who is now teaching at Lake Forest, and she is a home-maker who claimed to have "two other careers, each lasting less than a year." They were originally from New Orleans, and she especially had a true southern drawl and a contagious laugh.

Such is the joy of cruising, where people come together from dif-ferent walks of life and share their stories easily.

September 30, 1998

Up nice and early in time to bid farewell to our southern neighbors and Bob and Coleen, hoping we would see them again in Charleston.

We had decided to take a detour to the Outer Banks. We were able to sail a part of the way and were grateful for that, but we had now left the waterway (just when we were getting used to its particular naviga-tion), and the entrance to Manteo proved to be very confusing because two channels intersected, one from the sea and the entrance to Man-teo. A call to the Marina certainly saved the day as we made the right choice, and our berth is at the end of the dock with no other boats around. It felt almost as good as being anchored or moored.

October 1, 1998

The *Elizabeth 2,* a replica of the sixteenth-century sailing vessel, was in port, so we toured it. Oh, to think how those early settlers made it to the new world and the conditions they had to put up with is mind-boggling. Their courage and perseverance are awe-inspiring. I hope I can remember this when I begin to have a frustrating moment on land or sea.

We proceeded via bike to the Elizabethan Gardens, which was about three miles out of town and so worth the ride. How beautiful it is to sit and have lunch and meander through the glorious flowers and vegetation.

That night, the winds howled and gusted to about 30 knots, and we were grateful to the dock master for warning us to adjust our dock lines. We did, however, rock and roll all night, and by morning, we had to radio the dock master to help us disembark.

Back on land, we decided to take advantage of the marina courtesy car and headed to Nags Head, Duck, and Corolla. There, the Atlantic Ocean was a beautiful sight to behold. The beach was beautiful, but it was sad to see how built up it was. Quite a number of ostentatious homes packed tightly together with maybe a slight water view.

We treated ourselves to a delightful lunch at a beach restaurant and combed the beach for shells.

Meanwhile, back at the marina, the wind had died down considerably, and we prepared ourselves and *Perpetual* for a morning departure.

October 3, 1998

A beautiful bright morning, and we were off to sea again. It's always a thrilling feeling to get underway after a brief stay and head off for places unknown, at least to us.

Today, we were back on the Albemarle and on our way to the Alligator River, quietly wondering why the river had that name. Even though we couldn't sail, it was such a picturesque landscape of unspoiled wetland that we didn't mind.

Our destination was Tuckahoe Point, an anchorage off the Alligator River, and according to Jordan's guide, we were to "steer toward the tree in the water about 100 yards off Tuckahoe Point." There were quite a few trees, and the question of the day became, "Which tree?" We made a rough calculation of the middle tree and threw down the hook.

No alligator sightings so far.

It is Saturday evening, and another perfect sunset is about to occur at a beautiful anchorage. There are times when I think I must be dreaming this whole adventure! When we first began thinking of doing something different for this sabbatical year, we certainly had no idea that our journey through these waterways would be so beautiful and intriguing.

October 4, 1998

Today our plan is to take the Alligator Pungo River Canal, a twenty-one-mile land cut to Bellhaven. Again unable to sail much but enjoying the scenery.

Ann and I each take two-hour shifts at the helm. Following a compass course and watching the depth sounder demands concentration, and it's a quiet time for us both as I find myself in sort of a soothing reverie.

We are now towing the dinghy, and it's so much easier, and if it's slowing us down, I haven't noticed.

Our main destination is New Bern by Friday, where Ann's aunt and uncle live, and her brothers will be arriving for the family reunion.

We arrived at the Pungo Creek, where we set the anchor. Another sailboat is anchored close by, which is always a comforting sight. The clouds overhead were a bit disconcerting, and we were thankful to be in a protected harbor, as a major thunderstorm occurred as we were fixing dinner. The anchor held, and we had a cozy dinner down below.

October 5, 1998

Woke up to pea soup fog and waited it out for some visibility. We motor sailed most of the day. Our plan was to get diesel at the Mayo Company fuel dock, but we changed our minds as the place looked pretty deserted. We then opted for Gayle Creek to anchor for the night.

We approached ever so slowly as there were crab pots all over, and to get one caught in the prop would surely be a problem. Our next choice was Bonner Bay, even though the Waterway Guide gave a very vague description. When we found ourselves in five feet, we quickly retraced our course back to Gayle Creek, Crab pots and all. It was getting dark, so there was no time to be picky. We found a spot among the pots and hoped for the best. It was a rather secluded anchorage. We could spot a home on the shore with some life present, but other than that, we were alone with the crab pots.

October 6, 1998

Today was definitely the worst day we've had so far, and hopefully, it will never repeat itself.

As Ann struggled to pull up the anchor, she realized it was more difficult than usual and quickly remembered the dam crab pots. It took great perseverance and patience that ultimately freed us, and we carefully threaded our way to a crab pot free zone and headed off to Oriental, the sailing capital of North Carolina.

Today we would have to tackle what locals called the "naughty Neuse River." The Waterway Guide described it as "vying with the Albemarle producing the meanest water." The winds were blowing over twenty, so we were feeling some apprehension, especially when we hoisted the main to find a small tear. We decided to take the main down, thinking that the tear could get worse and accelerated the engine. All of a sudden, the engine started to lose power, and then nothing. We had just entered the Neuse River and were drifting aimlessly, but not for long as we pulled out the jib, and thankfully, the wind was just right for a downwind sail.

Four hours later, we were in Oriental Harbor and called Boat US, a member-based organization that we belong to specifically for towing if needed. The seas were rather choppy, and the wind hadn't subsided, so we were told to anchor until his arrival. It was with great effort and help from the Captain that we were able to free the anchor and eventually get towed in. "Ladies, you are on top of your game today," was our tow Captain's reply to us as we thanked him for his help.

What a welcome sight the marina was. We quickly contacted a mechanic who would be available in a couple of days.

For now, it just felt good to sit and do nothing. We had indeed tackled the Neuse and survived. We were now only a day's sail to New Bern for the family reunion.

October 7 and 8, 1998

Oriental is a particularly neat little town, especially for boaters in need of services. A ship's store was right across the street, and since we were having some difficulty flushing the head (toilet), it was important to be able to discuss the problem with a knowledgeable person who made the diagnosis and also had the part. After a few laborious hours, I completed the task with favorable results. A functioning head is a cruising necessity.

The sailmaker was just down the road, so off came the mainsail, and by the following day, it was repaired.

How fortunate for us to be in a port where everything was so accessible and efficient.

The mechanic arrived and spent four hours with me, showing me how to bleed the engine and change the fuel filters and oil. He decided it must have been a clogged fuel filter that caused the problem. *Perpetual* was back in commission again, and what a relief that was.

We purchased a Bruce anchor with twenty feet of chain, which should make anchoring more secure as we head south.

THE HAAS FAMILY REUNION, NEW BERN, NORTH CAROLINA

October 9, 1998

I felt somewhat tentative, leaving the slip as we hoped the engine would cooperate. The rain was falling heavily, so out came our slickers, and up went our bimini, an awning that covers the cockpit. The engine sounded and acted fine, and after four hours, we were at the swing bridge in New Bern. It opened quickly after a call on the radio, and there on the left was The Bridge Point Marina, where Ann's Uncle Frank had reserved our slip.

We actually made New Bern on the scheduled date that we had been talking about for the past eight weeks. What a feeling!!

After a quick shower, Ann's Uncles, Frank and Don, arrived and whisked us off to the Oktoberfest, where Aunt Barb, Uncle Frank's wife, was serving the food, and "We can't be late."

It was a typical church function with lots of Bavarian cuisine and accordion music. We are not used to so much activity, but hopefully, we'll adjust. Anyway, the family is very nice, and we were both thrilled to arrive at their sweet home and get more acquainted.

October 10, 1998

It felt strange sleeping in a single bed. I felt as if I would land on the floor during the night. I've gotten so used to our v-berth, which is totally enclosed on the sides, that I'll most likely need a crib when we get home.

Today, Rich and Marlene are arriving from New Jersey, and Ann's other brother, Tom, and his partner, Sara, from Charlottesville, North Carolina.

Uncle Don and I decided to play tennis before the partying began. He is an avid player and, for seventy years of age, is in awesome shape. We both had a great workout.

Meanwhile, back at the house, everyone had gathered, and it was great fun reuniting and catching up. Lots of wine, food, and laughter. Tom and Sara announced that they were getting married on March 21 in the Bahamas, so that will be a gala event. Marlene and Rich were thrilled that our last true grounding was with them weeks before our departure. Barb cooked a delicious Stroganoff, and everyone toasted everyone with great cheer.

October 11, 1998

Uncle Frank had made brunch reservations at the Marine Base. Since Tom, Sara, Marlene, and Rich were staying in the hotel at the marina, we swung by to pick them up. Frank decided that the men would go in one car and the women would ride with Barb, who we found out was one scary driver. We were all holding on to each other for dear life, laughing and joking, not wanting to show Barb our terror. The good news is that the brunch was fantastic, and we lived to digest it.

We bid farewell to Tom and Sara with hopes of seeing them in the Bahamas.

October 12, 1998

Rich, Marlene, Frank, and Don boarded *Perpetual* for a day of sailing on the Neuse. I felt a little nervous having so many people aboard, but thankfully, all went well, and everyone seemed to have a great time. The weather was lovely, and the winds were just right for everyone to experience the joy of sailing.

Back at the house, Barb prepared dinner, which we all enjoyed even though we (meaning Ann and I) were ready to fall asleep.

We said goodbye to Rich and Marlene, and I got a second wind as I told Don that he had great legs and he could be a model for a senior sports catalog. It could be a whole new career for him, and I could be his agent. We could do socks, shorts, and anything else he felt comfortable about. After all, I am a Gerontological Nurse Practitioner, and I know good legs when I see them. The laughter echoed throughout the house as Don just smiled, looking at me like I had a screw loose.

October 13, 1998

Don has left. He told Frank to say goodbye. I guess I scared the man half to death, but he did seem to enjoy the banter and attention. I hope I'm right about that.

Frank has just announced that he would like to accompany us on *Perpetual* for a few days, preferably to Jacksonville, Florida, where his daughter lives. Ann and I were aghast and momentarily stunned, unable to respond.

Finally, Ann said, "Uncle Frank, we won't be in Florida until late November."

Uncle Frank then said, "Well, how about six or seven days?"

He would like Ann and I to approach Barb with the idea. How to handle this became today's dilemma. We thought two days at the most would be doable, but beyond that, we would be stretching it. How do we graciously tell him?

When we talked with Barb, she was quite upset that he had "intruded himself on us." We assured her he had not (a small fib) and that we would love to have him on board for a couple of days, which she finally agreed to since she would have to pick him up.

Frank, although not completely thrilled, seemed relatively satisfied, and Ann and I put that dilemma to bed along with ourselves.

October 14, 1998

Uncle Frank was up quite early and wanted to get an early start. Our destination was Oriental, and we had a beautiful day sailing and motoring back down the Neuse. Uncle Frank was in his glory, telling us various stories from his days at sea.

We anchored in Oriental and dinghied into our favorite Ships Store, which I discovered only six days ago, in search of an extra shear pin for the dinghy engine. No luck, but I enjoyed the ride and purchased the needed ice.

Back on board, we fixed dinner while Uncle Frank attached a hook and eye to our hatch that can now be locked from the inside. Great idea!

Sitting in the cockpit enjoying a magnificent sunset put a nice end to our first day of sailing with Uncle Frank.

October 15, 1998

Frank was up on deck by the time we awoke. I hurriedly got the coffee going so we could get started. *Perpetual* is a small boat for three people, one of whom is over six feet tall. It was clear that Frank wanted to get underway. Our destination was Beaufort, North Carolina, where Barb would be meeting us.

Out on the ICW, we saw our first dolphins frolicking and actually following us for a while. Frank was at the helm, and we should have been paying more attention to him as he was trying to negotiate a range that we were approaching, almost steering *Perpetual* right into the marker. He admitted he had a hard time differentiating the colors of the markers but didn't want to relinquish the helm even though the depth sounder alarm would be screeching with four feet showing on the monitor. It was getting quite tense for Ann and I as we tried to guide him to slow down, and there were times I had to gently grab the wheel so we would keep on course.

After five nerve-wracking hours, we were safely anchored in Beaufort, and we dinghied in to meet Barb.

We enjoyed a delightful dinner as Frank enthusiastically talked about his two days sailing with the Anns' and it sounded like he truly enjoyed himself. Since that was the goal, we felt happy. We said our farewells with hopes of seeing each other on our return trip.

Back on board *Perpetual*, it was time to breathe a sigh of relief as two weary sailors crawled into their cozy v-berth.

October 16, 1998

We decided to take a recoup day and explore Beaufort, which is a very charming and interesting coastal town. Many of the boats where we are anchored, use this spot as a stopover before venturing out into the ocean for destinations like Bermuda, Spain, England, etc.

It was very relaxing just walking and visiting the various shops and basically just being quiet. It had been six days of being with people, and it was time to return to our simple life aboard *Perpetual*, and periods of silence were part of it.

October 17, 1998

Today, we left Beaufort and entered the Atlantic, our destination being Cape Lookout. It was somewhat nail-biting, coming out of the channel with the traffic of fishing boats and a large container ship entering. All went well, thank goodness. We had our compass course plotted from buoy six but ended up south of the land mass and had to correct and search for the intended buoy. It took longer than expected. We were now back in the ocean. The winds were blowing twenty, and the water was a beautiful blue-green, such a welcome change from brackish brown. Dolphins were on our bow diving in and out of the water, and pelicans were soaring overhead and plunging into the water to perhaps retrieve some lunch. We, on the other hand, hadn't eaten a morsel, our concentration being totally on the sea and its marvels and also trying to find the entrance buoy. We were fortunate to see a group of boats approaching the entrance and were happy to follow.

Safely anchored about a half mile off the beach, and even though it's not the calmest of anchorages, it is incredibly beautiful. We are actually tucked into a little hook with the ocean on the other side of a spit of land.

Tomorrow, we'll explore the beach, but for now, the wind echoes a slight howl, the stars are ever so clear, the glorious lighthouse casts its light every five seconds, and our trusty Bruce anchor is holding. Ann is sound asleep, and it seems like all is well with the world.

October 18, 1998

What a spectacular day! We dinghied onto the beach and found a path to the ocean that was lined with purple heather, seagrass, and goldenrod, and there, over the dunes, the majestic Atlantic Ocean with its blue-green water and the softest of white sand, very reminiscent of Fire Island in New York. However, we were alone with only a handful of fishermen surfcasting from the beach. It was heavenly as we sat on our towels, writing postcards and remarking that it doesn't get any better than this.

After lunch, we walked the beach to the lighthouse, which is very similar to Cape Hatteras, differentiated by diamonds instead of stripes. We had a pleasant conversation with the volunteer who runs the gift shop and actually lives there during the season. She is given accommodations and a small stipend and seems to love it. Who wouldn't?

As we dinghied back to the boat, we noticed there was only one other boat at anchor. It was Sunday, and most likely, everyone was heading back to work the next day. But lucky us, it seems like every day is Saturday, and every night is Friday night. Oh, how I love this life!

Tomorrow, we are off to Swansboro. It's about a thirty-five-mile trip. Our friend Joan, who is back in New York, insisted we call her niece, who lives in Emerald Isle, which is very close by. So we did, and she invited us for dinner tomorrow evening. How nice.

Our cabin is so cozy, with the candles glowing and the cool breeze blowing through the companionway. The brilliant stars are all over the sky, and I am feeling so grateful to be experiencing this very moment.

October 19, 1998

We got an early start and reluctantly left paradise. We decided to hug the shore more closely to see if we would come in closer to the inlet, which would prove our theory that the buoys had been re-numbered, and indeed, we were right.

With the following sea behind us, we surfed into the inlet and began the long trip down the Intracoastal. We would be entering Bogue Sound, and our Waterway Guide warned us of extreme shoals and to focus attention on the buoys ahead as well as astern. We set the depth alarm for eight feet and proceeded very carefully. By the time we arrived in Swansboro, we were pretty beat. It had been eight hours since we left Cape Lookout, and arriving at the marina, we went aground and got off quickly, thankfully, but that scraping sound is enough to put shivers down your spine every time.

We were very happy to have an invite for dinner. Dianne and her husband, Jack, picked us up and brought us to their adorable home. Ann has a cold, so it was doubly nice to sit in a warm house eating pork chops while enjoying pleasant conversation.

October 20, 1998

Had to back out from the dock, but it was high tide, and all went well. It is a gray and misty morning. We have our foul weather gear on and are ready for another day of pure concentration on depth and buoys. We have the alarm set for seven feet, and just when you think you are totally in the channel, the alarm screams otherwise, and you look behind, and you are out of the channel. It's so tricky, but the stark beauty of the secluded marshlands keeps us centered, I hope.

We had to call the Coast Guard to find out if there would be target practice at Camp Lejeune. If the light is red, we can not proceed and will have to wait an hour. As we approached, we could hear what sounded like bombs, but there was no red light. It was an eerie feeling but also exciting as we kept moving and, of course, maintaining a watchful eye on the buoys off the bow and stern and listening to the "bombs bursting in air" as Ann took cover on the cockpit floor. That four-mile stretch now behind us, Ann regained her seat in the cockpit as we both breathed a sigh of relief and had a hearty laugh, which always relieves tension.

Now it was bridge time, and this one had a scheduled opening time, and along with at least ten other boats, we would have to wait thirty minutes for the opening. Not an easy task, especially with a two to three-knot current, as we throttled forward to reverse and neutral endlessly, just to stay put and not hit another boat, as they did the same. It was quite dicey, but *Perpetual* performed beautifully.

We were so happy to pull into Harbor Village Marina with all its amenities, a sparkling clean boaters' lounge, and laundry, where we did three loads of wash while watching Oprah. Life is wonderful!

October 21, 1998

Today, we headed for Bald Head Island. Ann had read about this island last summer when she was at a conference in Atlanta and saved the article describing this beautiful place off the Cape Fear River, which is only accessible to land by ferry. The inhabitants use bikes and golf carts for transportation. It sounds great, and we are planning to stay for two or three days. Yea!

"Old Baldy" the Bald Head Island lighthouse

Back on the ICW, it was nice seeing sailboats behind us. We pulled out the jib, hoping it would give us an extra knot or get us to the bridge on time for the opening as I broke out in a song, "Get me to the bridge on time." We were a tad early and held back a bit so as not to be among the pack of boats awaiting the opening. When it finally opened, we were going full throttle because we had no idea how long it would stay open.

Ann radioed the bridge tender announcing our approach, and he replied, "Are you that little sailboat approaching?"

"Yes sir, roger that," was Ann's reply.

"Well, pick up your feet, captain, and bring her on through," and so we did.

In truth, we are one of the smallest boats out here, and it's noticeable, especially at marinas where other liveaboards can't believe we are liveaboards. However, our compact twenty-eight-foot sailboat is comfortable, cozy, and affordable and is providing us with the means of having this incredible adventure. She may be little, but she's taking us on a ride of a lifetime.

Now, back to the day's journey where we were entering Snow's Cut, which was reported to have swift currents and that it did, carrying us along with several other boats at a good pace and with the channel being quite narrow, we were getting too close for comfort even with constant forward and reverse action on the throttle. Finally, out on the Cape Fear River, at least the depth was twenty or more feet, but very confusing markings on the chart. There were a few boats ahead, and we decided to follow them. All seemed great for a while as we were now putting red to port and green to starboard until we came to green number one, which, if we were continuing on the Waterway, should now have been kept to port. It did have a yellow square, probably a clue we missed, and we continued following the lead boat who went aground, and we followed, with the trawler following us.

The trawler got off rather quickly, and so did we, thank goodness; however, the lead sailboat seemed pretty dug in. A couple of runabouts offered to try and pull them off, and we radioed them to see if we could be of assistance, but they assured us they were fine and would wait for high water.

We were now in deep water; however, we were a bit clueless as to where Bald Head Marina was. In the distance, we spotted the lighthouse, Old Baldy, headed toward it and followed the buoys into the breakwater, which surfed us into an absolutely beautiful marina.

Sometimes, I truly believe we are being guided by something greater than ourselves. Maybe because we are. We were thrilled to be safe and sound, and what a bonus it was to be at this glorious spot.

October 22, 1998

As I look back at what I've written and how I often say, "It can't get any better than this," and somehow it does. Each harbor has its own surprises, its own unique beauty, but it's also the amazing gift of being in the moment, the present that is so exhilarating, exciting, and sometimes terrifying but is giving me this feeling of aliveness that I hope I can always carry with me.

Frying Pan Shoals

Here we are on this magnificent island that started development in 1983 by the Mitchell family, and they clearly have done a tasteful job in preserving its two thousand acres, building Cape Cod-type homes. What is so wonderful is that ten thousand acres of salt marsh creeks have been deeded to North Carolina to be left undeveloped.

On our bikes, we were off to explore. No cars are allowed on the island, only golf carts. We fastened our tennis rackets onto our carriers and toted the required tennis shorts since the weather was rather cool and we were now wearing sweats.

Our first destination was Cape Fear and Frying Pan Shoals. After coming to an end on the road, we parked our bikes and trekked through the sand with the mighty Atlantic exploding its waves to starboard. We finally arrived at Cape Fear, and we were the only people there; however, a dead dolphin was lying on the beach. So sad! We had just read that this area was called the "Graveyard of the Atlantic" as the shoals had shipwrecked many boats, and perhaps that's what happened to the poor dolphin. It was a somber moment as we gazed out into the powerful, sometimes deadly ocean.

On the way back, we changed into our tennis gear and found magnificent tennis courts adjacent to a golf course. There was even a croquet area. It was great fun playing tennis and getting some real exercise.

Back at the marina, we met a lovely woman named Laura, who lived on the island with her husband for the past year. They had just purchased a 1969 Pearson 35 that had been completely redone and sold their home so she could live out her dream of living on a sailboat for a year. She related that her husband was not as thrilled about the idea. We invited her to come aboard *Perpetual*, also manufactured by Pearson, to see our humble surroundings and tell her a bit about our trip thus far. Her plan is to go to the Bahamas, leaving sometime in November. We promised to visit her boat tomorrow.

It is quite cool down below, so we battened down the hatches and had an early night bundled up in our down comforter.

October 23, 1998

It was so cold, we could see our breath, and leaving the down comforter was so hard since we didn't have heat on the boat. The temperature plummeted to thirty-six degrees last night.

A nice hot cup of coffee got us started, and we were off to the grocery store.

A few large power boats arrived, and they wanted to be together, and we were in one of the slips. Ann told them we would move to accommodate their request. I, on the other hand, was feeling annoyed having to undo our lines, etc. I got over it quickly, however, and backed out and into our new slip. A pissy moment all gone.

Today, we explored the village center, which included a most beautiful chapel that provides services every Sunday, given by traveling clergy. The windows overlooked the marshlands, and the interior was exquisite, with lots of oak and wainscotting. There was a post office, but it was closed, and a nice town hall with inviting rocking chairs on its porch. Old Baldy stood in the center and was open for a climb. Ann declined, but I had to go to the top, all one hundred and eight steps. I was all alone and felt a bit nervous, but the view was incredible. I could see Southport, Frying Pan Shoals, and even *Perpetual* sitting calmly at the marina. Our last stop was to a quaint gift store where we purchased another sailboat ornament to hang on our Christmas tree.

Back at the marina, we packed up our bikes and stopped to see Laura's boat *Hornpipe*. We were quite impressed with her upgrades, especially since it's almost thirty years old. We planned to possibly see Laura in Charleston.

It's not as cold tonight, and we can put the screens back in the hatch instead of closing everything up. The wind is calmer, too, and we are heading south—YES!

October 24, 1998

Out of the inlet, we were told to gun the engine because of the stiff currents, so we did, and it worked. We found the ICW in spite of the chart and trekked down the ditch, which is a common name boaters use for the Intracoastal Waterway. There were beautiful blue skies overhead and a hint of cool fall air that challenged our wardrobe selection every few hours. We intended to anchor but decided to head into Myrtle Beach Yacht Club so we could check emails. Golf courses are everywhere as we motored our way to a very accommodating club.

It was great getting Jordan's email, which said he was successful in finding a flight from Amsterdam to Miami. It looks like all our kids will be with us for Christmas. Two months from today is Christmas Eve. We are psyched!

October 25, 1998

Today, we motored through the part of the ditch that is supposed to be the least appealing and also rather hazardous, thirty-five miles of a rather narrow land cut with a three-mile area called the rock pile.

It definitely held our concentration, and by the time we were ready to anchor, we were exhausted. Prince Creek was not going to fit the bill as it was too narrow and too deep. Happily, we found Cow House Creek and anchored *Perpetual* in eight feet, surrounded by marshland on one side and a wooded forest on the other.

Time to celebrate with a magnificent Sunday dinner, chicken, potatoes, gravy, and salad.

October 26, 1998

What a gift to wake up on a Monday morning and not have to think about work.

The cabin is brisk, to say the least, but layered up as we are, it's bearable, and the good news is, we are in the same spot. I woke twice and checked during the night to make sure.

We are sitting here in the absolute stillness of the morning. The mist over the water is just starting to burn off; the sky is a brilliant blue, and we both keep saying how grateful we are.

We finally picked up the anchor and headed off to Georgetown. No wind to speak of, and we motored the whole way. There was not a boat in sight for miles, and then all of a sudden, out of the blue, it looked like the "Love Boat" approaching from astern. We quickly headed starboard so the "Nantucket Clipper," a 207 ft ship, could pass with passengers waving at two surprised sailors.

We arrived in Georgetown, South Carolina in mid-afternoon and set the hook along with several other boats right off the town dock.

It's always fun exploring a new harbor, and this little town was quite attractive. It had a pleasant harbor walk promenade and lots of interesting shops and restaurants. The paper and steel mill factories were a bit of an eyesore with their black smoke and pungent odor emitting from the stacks. The people we spoke to, however, felt this was part of life here as it provided many with good jobs. I just wondered about their health.

October 27, 1998

We carefully lowered our bikes into the dinghy, and off we went to explore Georgetown. We found the grocery store outside of the town and then stopped and had a nice lunch at the "Rice Paddy." We hadn't treated ourselves to lunch since Manteo, so we were due.

We had a large number of groceries, so I decided to make two trips with the dinghy. As luck would have it, the tow line got caught in the prop, and the pin broke AGAIN! So we rowed the bikes back and, after loading everything onto the boat, realized the anchor rode seemed caught around the keel. My initial thought was we'd have to find a diver; however, after much maneuvering and Ann's brilliant idea to turn the boat back upwind since the strong current had turned it. It was rather difficult, to say the least, but we finally freed the anchor line and reset her. It was actually dark now, and a gentleman in a trawler yelled over to us, asking if we were ok, and then exclaimed that we were "working too hard and should be having cocktails in the cockpit." So we did—Chardonnay followed by leftover chicken and peas, so delicious.

LOWCOUNTRY OF SOUTH CAROLINA

October 28, 1998

We left Georgetown around nine. Another beautiful day, cool with five to ten knots, tried the jib sail, but with winding land cuts and very shallow areas, we pulled her in and motored, concentrating heavily on buoys and depth.

We now have many ranges to negotiate. These are fixed navigation aids that have to be lined up when in a channel; otherwise, you will go aground. They are extremely helpful, but it takes some practice to line them up, and lining them up is not optional. We did two and were very proud of this new accomplishment.

We were now in the Lowcountry of South Carolina, with vast marshlands and barely any trees, and the tea-colored water had changed to grayish green. The whole picture is starkly beautiful.

We arrived at our planned anchorage, and the setting was magnificent. Two other boats were already there, and other than that, it was totally secluded except for the birds nesting in the tall sea grass.

And then the most thrilling sunset—this pink-orange ball descended into the marsh, leaving the pinkest sky imaginable. We were so awe-struck, and as a bonus, two dolphins appeared on our bow. Exquisite beauty au natural, what a wonderful life this is!

October 29, 1998

When we awoke, the two other boats had left, and the thought crossed our minds. Oh boy, maybe we, too, should have left earlier; perhaps they know something we don't.

Since we were now heading into big tides and heavy currents, we were feeling a bit concerned. We had a tide schedule but were unsure about the currents. It would be high tide in the afternoon, so we had the depth sounder set for eight feet as we headed for Charleston Harbor. It was another cloudless blue sky day. The Waterway Guide described that it could be difficult to enter the harbor with the heavy currents. One look at the chart convinced us to plot compass courses between buoys as the guide recommended. Ann diligently plotted the courses as I concentrated on maintaining them.

We could see the outline of the city of Charleston, South Carolina, and felt very excited. We hadn't seen a large city since Norfolk, Virginia, and to our surprise, the water was so calm. We could see the intended buoys without binoculars and had a relaxing entrance into the harbor.

We arrived at the marina earlier than expected and took a moment to congratulate ourselves and quietly thank God for making it to Charleston, South Carolina. The marina showers would be first on our to-do list as we hadn't had that luxury in days. Following that, we did the wash. It was now time to take a bike ride into downtown Charleston.

Riding our bikes next to the thruway was quite challenging, having gotten used to country roads, but very well worth it as the downtown is lovely. We found a nice Italian restaurant and enjoyed a delicious meal.

Back on *Perpetual,* we called our friend Jeanne, who is planning on flying to Savannah from New York in two weeks, to join us for a few days of sailing. This seemed like a great idea when we initiated the plan. Hopefully, it will be fun sharing the joys and realities of our current lives; I only hope she thinks so.

October 30, 1998

Talking with people at the marina is always fun, but it is especially nice when you see people you've met prior. Across from us was a couple we had met briefly in Elizabeth City, Cathy and Warren from Canada aboard their trawler *Irish Mist.* A trawler is a powerboat much quicker than *Perpetual*, and we wondered how they arrived at the same time as us. Well, it so happens that Warren remained in Belhaven, North Carolina, for three weeks while Cathy flew home because she was homesick. Warren related, "This is going to be one expensive year."

Art and Jane are another couple we met in Charleston. Ann encountered Art on the dock early one morning, and they exchanged stories about their trip experiences. Later that day, while walking up to the marina along one of the narrow docks, we found ourselves following a woman riding a small bike. As the three of us were approaching a sharp turn to the right, the woman appeared to misjudge the turn, and the front wheel of her bike went off the dock, plunging both bike and biker into the shallow water. Fortunately, she fell off the bike close to the dock, and we were able to reach out and help her climb back on a nearby ladder and sit down on one of the small benches. Although she insisted she was OK, she looked horridly pale and seemed quite shaken. Meanwhile, another onlooker had called EMS, for which we were grateful. In quick order, they determined she had sustained no injury and left the scene, which gave us the opportunity to introduce ourselves and learn that she was Art's wife, Jane. As we helped her to her boat, her major concern post-incident was the surprise party she'd planned for Art's 70th birthday that night, for which she had ordered a spread of food and drink from Harris Teeter, an upscale local supermarket. She wanted to reschedule the party for the next night. We promised to take care of it for her and insisted that she lie down. "Please come to the party tomorrow night at the dock house. We assured her we would be there.

As we rode our bikes to Harris Teeter, we each reflected on what just happened. We were both a tad shook up ourselves, thinking about how different the outcome could have been. Mostly, though, the incident underscored how, in our present waterway world, complete strangers can so quickly and easily become trusted and valued friends, even if we have no idea whether our paths will ever cross again.

October 31, 1998

Happy Halloween and another beautiful day in Charleston as we took off on our bikes to find West Marine. We wanted to get a small mushroom anchor that we could attach to our regular anchor line, which would hopefully prevent the line from getting caught on the keel. We learned that West Marine was further than we were willing to bike, so we locked them to a telephone pole and hopped on the bus. We actually had to transfer to another bus that eventually got us there.

In the checkout line, we met a fellow boater named Mike, who actually lives in Charleston and insisted on driving us back to where our bikes were parked. We were quite happy to take him up on his offer.

Back at the marina, we attended the birthday party and had a very enjoyable evening, meeting some new people commiserating about adventures at sea and celebrating Halloween. Jane had recovered and was very grateful for our help. There is something special about this boating community, and we feel so blessed to be part of it.

November 1 and 2, 1998

We decided to see more of Charleston by bike. We biked all over, riding past gorgeous pastel-colored homes located on the waterfront, with its scenic parks. Then, onward to the bustling market area, with its various vendors selling food and crafts. After that, we found Meeting Street in the French Quarter, which reminded us of Greenwich Village in New York. We even found a dinner movie theater. Since it was now getting late, we tethered our bikes to a pole and opted to see *Saving Private Ryan* while eating chicken wings and sipping Chardonnay; not an easy movie to watch while eating.

All in all, we loved Charleston and will definitely visit again on our return trip.

November 3, 1998

Waking up late caused a bit of morning mayhem. Our intended time had been 6 a.m. as we wanted to leave the harbor at high tide. We were now an hour late, so we hurriedly put on the coffee and donned our foul-weather gear as it was cool and rainy.

As we pulled out into the harbor, we realized we had a bascule bridge to contend with, and it didn't open till nine, and it was only a mile away. We hadn't checked the guide last eve so hence we would spend an hour waiting. Another lesson learned the hard way.

There were a few boats in front of us as the bridge opened. As we approached, we heard the gears cranking, and the bridge started coming down. I don't know if she didn't see us or was being a smart ass; nevertheless, we made it through with full throttle and breathed a sigh of relief, but not for long as we were heading into Elliott Cut with its swift currents that felt like white water rafting. We were behind three sailboats, and we were all fighting pretty hard to stay in the middle as there were lots of rocks on the sides. It was only about a mile long, but a memorable body of water, that's for sure.

We were now in the Stono River, still part of the ICW, and had our eyes peeled on the depth sounder. It was unbelievably shallow in spots, and somehow, the depths on the charts were not in agreement with what we were experiencing. Behind us, a sailboat went aground, and then we followed. Luckily, though, we were able to free ourselves, but not without tattered nerves. As we approached the South Edison River, the alarm went off at six feet again, followed by moments of frenzy. Sometimes, this just isn't fun.

We finally anchored, only to realize that because of the current, we were now over the anchor. Absolutely exhausted, we reset the anchor, and thank God it held. We were the only boat around.

I was down below when we heard a dinghy coming toward our boat. Someone who sounded inebriated asked Ann for a match. "I will see if my husband has one." I promptly found a pack to give him as I hid in the head. Cohansey River deja vu, no, not tonight, we can't cope!

He seemed satisfied and sped away. We had a quick supper. Ann watched the midterm election results as I crawled into the cozy v-berth and found comfort just waiting for sleep to arrive.

November 4, 1998

At least we feel well rested, and the anchor not only held, but our new little mushroom attachment seems to be helping. So off to another six hours of eyes glued to the depth and hands firmly set on the wheel. After yesterday, we felt a bit tentative, but as the saying goes, no pain, no gain. We must be brave and face those monster shoals with tenacious courage—sounds good.

The weather was cloudy and cool, and the trip was thankfully without incident. When we made the wide berth turn into the Coosaw River at red buoy 186, we were almost euphoric with the depths of twenty-five to thirty feet of water. It was time to see if we remembered how to sail. It was a blissful two hours of joy, and we remembered why we bought a sailboat.

It was about 2 p.m. when we arrived at Dataw Island Marina, which looks really nice. We'll stay put for a couple of days. The weather is supposed to really cool down.

November 5, 1998

Brrrr, it's quite cold, and we brought out our down comforter last night, which kept us fairly warm. After some hot coffee, we were off to tour the island.

It was interesting biking around and finding out that it was Alcoa Aluminum who began development on this barrier island in the early eighties. We rode past beautiful homes meticulously landscaped amongst huge oak trees with Spanish moss lazily hanging from their branches. Most homes have views of the pristine golf course or the scenic bay, which is a little too perfect for our tastes but nevertheless, a pleasant way to spend the day.

Back at the marina, the wind was blowing hard, but it was comforting to be tied securely to the floating dock. Tomorrow, we'll leave for Beaufort, so we reviewed the charts, ate dinner, wrapped ourselves in blankets, and finished a game of Scrabble we had started earlier. And to my surprise, I won by three points only because Ann got stuck with the Q as she lamented.

November 6, 1998

Beautiful blue skies, quite brisk, and some chop to the seas, but we were off to another day of watchful concern but gorgeous scenery. I never tire of the low country of South Carolina.

We pulled into Beaufort early afternoon, and what a treat to see *Lady Jane* at the adjacent dock and walking towards us were Karl and Patty, who we had met at Art's birthday party in Charleston. We welcomed them aboard and had some wine and cheese, exchanging lots of stories. It's amazing how at home you feel with people you have just met. Perhaps the common bond of living this mysterious, magical, sometimes miraculous life provokes the feeling. In any case, it's so very nice.

November 7, 1998

We met Karl and Patty for breakfast at a cute little cafe in Beaufort and bid our farewell for now as they were leaving for Hilton Head. Since they actually live in Beaufort, North Carolina, their trip south would go as far as Savannah and then home to Beaufort. We hoped to see them again on our return trip. However, I don't want to think about returning home right now.

Our new friend Michael, who we met at West Marine in Charleston, has called and is driving down with his partner Gus to visit. We met for lunch and had a delightful afternoon biking all around Beaufort. We found the house where they filmed "The Big Chill," and later, Michael brought us to a charming neighborhood development where the new homes resemble old Charleston southern homesteads, nestled in picturesque landscapes overlooking the water. Michael is a landscape architect and needed to check it out for a project he was working on.

Now, about Mike and Gus: Gus lives in New York City. They each take turns commuting every two weeks to see each other. They have been together for eleven years and love their arrangement. They are wonderful together, and it was such a treat to share the afternoon with them. We exchanged phone numbers and planned to meet again in the future, and somehow, I know we will.

November 8, 1998

A morning spent washing the boat, waxing the hull, and doing some touch-ups to the teak gave us some energy. After lunch, we found a tennis court and belted the ball around, which felt so good. Ann's game is improving a lot, and it's fun to hit with her.

Back to the boat for some leftovers.

November 9, 1998

Woke up to cold, rainy weather. Originally, we had planned to leave the marina and anchor just outside, but after listening to the weather and learning a cold front was supposed to arrive the next day, we decided we should leave for Hilton Head while the wind was calmer. So we did and had a pleasant trip, even sailing a bit as the showers gave away to bright sunshine.

We pulled into Palmetto Bay Marina, which was pretty packed and not as nice as some but adequate for a couple of days. Ann's niece is doing an architecture internship here, so it will be nice to see her.

November 10, 1998

Today our plan was to find a much-needed Beauty Salon for some haircuts.

Riding bikes in Hilton Head is particularly challenging with lots of cars and not enough traffic lights. I was so happy to spot a salon where we could park our bikes and spend a couple of hours relaxing.

We made it back to the marina just in time to meet Beth for dinner. She is thoroughly enjoying her internship and has a lovely apartment right across from the marina.

It was an early evening as she had to go back to work, and it was good for us as we are usually in a prone position by 8:15.

November 11, 1998

We were contemplating leaving today but decided to get the oil changed since the marina had a mechanic on site.

Ann did tons of washing while I supervised the oil change and wrote letters. While doing the laundry, Ann met a nice guy from Rhode Island who had sailed in. It took him five days from Norfolk, true blue water sailing. In 1989, he sailed around the world and spent three years doing it. He is retired, and it sounds like he can well afford both life on land and at sea. Since he rented a car, he offered to take us shopping, and what a treat not having to bike in the traffic. It was a very pleasant ride as he recounted his amazing journey around the world. We found a shopping mall and stocked up on food as he did the same. People on the water are just so helpful and interesting to boot.

Back on *Perpetual*, with the laundry all done, Ann was preparing a pre-Thanksgiving feast: chicken, potatoes, gravy, string beans, and stuffing. We dined by candlelight and enjoyed every morsel, watching Jeopardy.

November 12, 1998

Ann truly wanted to visit Daufuskie Island which is right across the Calibogue Sound from Hilton Head. I, however, had some concerns as I had read about the alligators and copperhead snakes that also reside there. We had some time to kill before heading to Savannah, so we decided to take a chance and off to Daufuskie we went.

As we approached the dock, we hailed the dock master, but no reply. There were only a few small boats and one mega yacht, so we decided to tie up and explore. We found the dockmaster dressed in an almost military-type attire who informed us that the Melrose Landing, which we had been hailing, was bought by a corporation that was developing parts of the island and was now called the Daufuskie Island Club and Resort. Bottom line: we could tie up for eighty cents a foot daily.

Out came our bikes as it was time to explore this island, which is only five miles long and two and a half miles wide. The beautiful tall oaks draped with moss-lined our ride as I wondered silently about the snakes and alligators that could be lounging in the thick vegetation. Best not to think about that now. We went from passing very rustic-type shacks to a beautiful resort community with gorgeous homes overlooking the ocean or golf course. We met a real estate woman who offered to give us a tour of the island tomorrow and visited the General Store, where we found the New York Times with today's date.

So glad we didn't let the snakes and alligators deter us from coming here. Back on *Perpetual*, we marveled at another beautiful sunset.

November 13-15, 1998

We had noticed water under the floorboards in the cabin, so we decided to take them out and lay them on the dock to dry. Since *Perpetual* has a very shallow bilge, water collects easily. We then realized our hand held bilge pump wasn't working. Since we had a 12:30 appointment with the realtor we met yesterday, we put that project on hold and hurriedly made an attempt to make ourselves look somewhat presentable.

We spent an enjoyable afternoon with Norma, who has lived on the island for eight years in a rather upscale community, as we later found out. She showed us many areas that were owned by the natives of the island who were descendants of the freed slaves and spoke Gullah, a combination of native African and southern English dialects. Their homes were quite sparse in comparison to the homes in the new community, but she felt it was the mixture and history of the island that made it so unique.

We stopped on the rustic side of the island to visit a potter and his wife. Beside his home was a twenty-eight-foot sailboat sitting on a cradle, which he and his wife had crossed the Atlantic on four different times. We talked about sailing for a while as he diligently created a beautiful pot.

Norma then took us to a beautiful property, one in particular overlooking the 18th hole of a pristine golf course that bordered the ocean. Ann was totally captivated. Yes, it was beautiful, but we were in no position to buy land presently, and so we got into a minor tiff. Suffice it to say after a good night's sleep, we came to an agreement that no check would be written, and yes, it's ok to think out of the box.

We were deep into disassembling the bilge when Norma arrived with a basket of fruit. She thought we could benefit from Vitamin C. Maybe we are showing signs of scurvy. She also arranged for us to play tennis. Oh my, she must be hoping that she has a potential sale. We thanked her for all her kindness and told her we would stop by her office after tennis.

After our successful bilge pump reassembly, we hopped on our bikes and found the tennis courts. It was delightful just belting the ball around, especially with our new property right across the road. Now, I had gotten smitten with the idea, but alas, we told Norma that we had a lot to think about and thanked her for her generosity. Secretly, we both knew this was not the time.

SAVANNAH, GEORGIA, MOON RIVER, AND CUMBERLAND ISLAND

November 15, 1998

We are on our way to Savannah, Georgia. Our destination is the Hyatt. As we approached the Savannah River, we hit a shoal, but in a few moments, we were off, and what a relief to now be in depths of forty to fifty feet. Even the busy river traffic didn't bother us.

We arrived at the Hyatt, and Ann had to secure the lines as the dock master was off, we later found out. It was challenging as the current was fierce, but all went well, or maybe we are just getting better at it.

Now safely docked, we took in the splendor of our new environment with a beautiful indoor swimming pool, workout room, and showers.

We had a wash to do and found a laundromat on the outskirts of this quaint historic downtown. Jeanne will be arriving tomorrow. This will be a wonderful couple of days exploring Savannah with her.

November 16, 1998

We hurriedly found a cab and did our provisioning before Jeanne's arrival. By the time she came, all was ready for a festive lunch as we hugged and chatted incessantly about anything and everything. After Jeanne got settled in her little stateroom, we were off to tour Savannah.

Ann had just finished the book "Midnight in the Garden of Good and Evil" and was thrilled to see Monterey Square, where the Mercer home is located. (Johnny Mercer wrote Moon River). There was a tour being offered that incorporated the story the book tells and weaved it into the history of Savannah. We decided to book a tour for tomorrow.

Tonight, we were off to the Pink House, a place Jeanne's parents had raved about when they visited it years ago. She insisted it was her treat, and it was spectacular!

Jeanne seems to be enjoying herself as much as we are, but it's only day number one.

November 17, 1998

Jeanne said she slept well in her cramped little quarters even though we rocked and rolled most of the night as the big container ships passed by. I'll admit to being tired and maybe a little hungover as we stayed up till the wee hours of the morning playing guitar and practicing "Moon River." It was a must, however, as we will be passing Moon River.

We met the tour bus at 9:30 and spent a fascinating three hours hearing about and seeing all the historic squares and homes that make this city so enchanting. The plot of the book was revealed, and I decided it was a must-read. We ended the tour by walking around Bonaventure cemetery, where Mr. Mercer is buried. We found a quaint tearoom for lunch, followed by a house tour, and went back to the Hyatt to ready ourselves to go see Emma Kelly, the lady of 6000 songs, performing at Hannah's. She was also featured in the book.

Wow, she was spectacular. She played the piano by memory with no music and sang beautifully. Jeanne and I had to sample a martini called Moon River, which had some blue liquor in it and tasted rather nice despite Ann's comments that it looked like mouthwash. She opted for a glass of Chardonnay. All in all, it was a wonderful evening.

Tomorrow, we leave Savannah with such fond memories and an autographed CD of Emma's songs.

November 18, 1998

At this special moment, we are anchored in a secluded creek with the Gay Men's chorus echoing their melodious voices through the marshlands. No words can describe this adequately; perhaps the word mystical? Sitting here in the cockpit with some cheese and crackers and a glass of wine as we watch the sun go down feels beyond mystical. Such a contrast from my mood this morning.

We left Savannah early and were motoring down the river with those large container ships, sometimes right next to us, when Jeanne asked if we could stop for coffee. I couldn't believe it, so I shot Ann a look as I silently thought that this part of the trip might be more challenging than we had planned. Alas, I agreed, and we pulled into a gas dock as Jeanne and Ann scurried off to find coffee, which they did, and I got $5 worth of diesel. Ok, it was only an hour, and we were on our way again.

Leaving Savannah

The morning was cool, but by afternoon, it warmed up for a stretch and then became oh-so windy, gusts up to 25 knots. We had the genoa up alone and were doing 5 knots, and at one point, we donned our life jackets as we entered a tricky inlet with the wind behind us and a following sea. Ann wasn't a happy sailor, but Jeanne and I loved it as we surfed the waves, and Jean kept saying, "I think I'm a natural."

Back to the present, dinner is served: Beef stroganoff. What a way to spend an evening!

November 19, 1998

We left the anchorage at nine and already had the main hoisted. Jeanne took the helm with some minor instructions at St Catherine's Sound. We agreed she could be a natural. We managed to sail for a period of time, which was a gift. Today, we found Moon River as Ann took the helm, and Jeanne and I took turns playing the guitar and crooning with tears streaming down our faces. It was A MOMENT. Jeanne has decided to send a telegram to Legal Aid, where she works as a lawyer, stating, "I'm not coming back, I may be a natural."

We anchored in New Tea Kettle Creek, and three little barges that we named the triplets joined us. Music and laughter echoed from *Perpetual* as we reminisced about the day.

November 20, 1998

Woke up to pea soup fog and waited till it lifted before we picked up the anchor. Today would be a day of ranges, at least twelve, and we hoped we were ready. They are very counterintuitive, as we explained to Jean, and demand full attention.

What an exhilarating day this was. Jeanne has become our disk jockey, having brought a plethora of CDs and choosing them to fit the occasion. As we were navigating both front and back ranges, Gene Autrey's "Back in the Saddle Again" was blasting from our speakers, with our melodious voices chiming in, "riding the range once more." Then there was the Lanier Bridge that Jeanne took us under without incident for our destination of Saint Simons Island, again proclaiming, "I'm a natural."

Safely docked at Golden Isle Marina with two ranges guiding us in because of a very shallow approach, it was definitely Miller Time.

Jeanne at the helm

We were all feeling excited by the day but also a little sad as this was Jeanne's last day of sailing with us. However, now that we know she's a natural, we'll have to plan another rendezvous.

We found a sweet cafe for dinner and toasted our three days of successful sailing in Georgia.

November 21, 1998

We all decided to take a tour of Saint Simons Island via trolley. I dozed through most of it, as these late nights are a challenge.

Jeanne insisted on taking us to dinner at a restaurant in town with a piano bar. It was such a treat, even though we all felt a little sad after such a perfect week.

November 22, 1998

Farewell to Jeanne for now, as she wants to meet us on our return trip. She left her Gay Men's CD with a note telling us, "Stay out of my room." I guess she truly enjoyed herself and wanted ownership of her bunk. It's amazing how the week worked out so well in spite of my reservations.

Ann and I poked around doing laundry, writing, and reading. We gradually got back to our routine and found ourselves all tucked in by eight.

November 24, 1998

Every time we say it can't get better than this, it somehow does or at least matches it. We are currently sitting at anchor in Cumberland Island, a small island owned by the Federal Government, and most of it has been preserved as a national park. It is only accessible by pleasure boat or ferry. We had recently heard of it because John Kennedy Jr. got married here in 1996.

We ferried our bikes via dinghy and began a day of exploration, riding on a small dirt path through a tropical forest of Palmettoes, Palms, Cypress, and the mighty oaks, forming a canopy of shade for the ride. We were totally in awe of the beauty before us and then over the dunes, the blue Atlantic with its seventeen miles of undeveloped beach. Not another human in sight, just us two, as we stopped and ate our picnic lunch mostly in silence, feeling so blessed to have discovered this unspoiled piece of paradise. After lunch, we took a bike ride on the hard-packed sand, which was thrilling. On our ride back to the dinghy, we found the Dungeness Ruins, where a grand mansion once stood that had been owned by the wealthy Carnegie family.

Back on *Perpetual*, we again marveled at all the beauty that was constantly unfolding.

ARRIVAL IN FLORIDA

November 24, 1998

It's hard to believe that tomorrow is Thanksgiving. Ann had a great idea: to find a soup kitchen or Church and ask if we could volunteer and serve. It will keep us focused on the true meaning of Thanksgiving and distract us from missing everyone. It would mean leaving Cumberland Island and traveling ten miles to Fernandina Beach, Amelia Island.

After the shortest day on the water, two hours, we crossed into Florida. What a feeling! We actually made it to Florida after a hundred days at sea, and it truly was Miller Time. So after we were safely docked, we toasted each other with a Bloody Mary and called the Methodist Church, and yes, we could help with dinner tomorrow.

Fernandina Beach, a city on Amelia Island, is all decorated for Christmas and looks so festive. We biked three miles down to the actual beach just to have a peek and then on to the Winn Dixie food market for some necessities.

It's a small world. When we arrived at the dock earlier, a gentleman took our lines and exclaimed what a coincidence to have two boats from East Hampton, NY. We later found out he had also purchased his boat from Three Mile Harbor as we did, but now his boat hailed Kings Point. I then told him we spent our first night at Kings Point Maritime Academy, and he revealed he had just retired from the Academy. Yes, he knew Captain John Hagedorn very well. It was great talking with John that evening and sharing this coincidental story.

We spent most of the evening calling family and wishing everyone Thanksgiving greetings. We both feel so thankful for our lives and health and for having made this journey thus far. This will be a memorable Thanksgiving; I just know it.

November 26, 1998, Thanksgiving

Here we are, drinking our morning coffee and watching the parade on our tiny television. The weather looks cool and rainy in NY, and here it's a pure blue sky with just enough breeze to keep the pesky gnats away.

After breakfast, we meandered down to the Methodist Church, where we were greeted warmly by the volunteers who had created an absolutely wonderful feast. At 1 p.m., people started arriving. Ann served turkey, and I piled potatoes on plates. Next to me was Trish, who had a wonderful sense of humor and had us laughing as she dished out the sweet potatoes with such spirit. She later confided that she had been a homeless alcoholic in the past and was so grateful for her current life, and now "Jesus was the only man in my life." She was very inspiring, as were many others whom we met when we finished serving and were invited to have dinner.

Back on *Perpetual*, we talked about the day, feeling so happy to have been part of this special Thanksgiving.

November 27, 1998

At 7 a.m., in Fernandina Beach, the shops opened, and discounts would be given to all who came in pajamas. Ann and I had long tee shirts on since that's what we sleep in; however, I don't think we really made the cut.

It was absolutely hysterical, with people in their elegant Victoria's Secret sleepwear and others wearing rollers in their hair and long or short flannel nightgowns in all different shapes and sizes. The town was certainly bustling with joy and laughter as Christmas music echoed through the shops. What a stark contrast to the malls in New York, where crowds are pushing and shoving to get bargains.

After beaching in the afternoon, we returned to the boat for a nice dinner of leftovers. We had originally planned to go out for dinner, but the truth is we prefer being on the boat.

November 28, 1998

Said farewell to Captain Perry and his wife. They were kind enough to give us their card and told us to call them if we needed anything when we got to CoCoa Beach. We have collected many cards along the way; however, we are cardless.

We were now off to Jacksonville Beach to meet up with Ann's cousin Nancy, Uncle Frank's daughter.

The weather feels more tropical now that we are in sunny Florida. Arrived at the marina just in time for an end-of-the-month party, free wine, and appetizers. We met a nice elderly couple who have a Pearson 35 and shared stories as we consumed quantities of veggies and dip. They are living on their boat and plan on spending the winter in the Bahamas.

Back on *Perpetual*, it was an early night, and that always feels good.

November 29, 1998

Ann's cousin Nancy arrived at noon. After getting reacquainted, she told us that her Mom had a heart attack two weeks after we left. We felt terrible and immediately expressed our concern that perhaps the whole reunion may have been too much for her. Nancy assured us that both her parents had the time of their lives. We gave Barb a quick call, and she insisted she was feeling well.

Over lunch, Ann and Nancy reminisced about their childhoods. It was great fun meeting Nancy, and I hoped we would see her again on our return trip.

November 30, 1998

It's unbelievable to be sitting here in St Augustine, anchored off the city with Christmas lights dotting the harbor. It's 5:40 in the evening, the sun has just gone down, and the weather is warm and balmy. No gnats for a change, so sitting on deck is a treat. It feels strange coming from New York to experience such warm weather during the Christmas season. However, I do love warm weather, and I do love Christmas, so this year, I can make it work.

We left Jacksonville Beach early this morning to be with the high tide and had an enjoyable motor passage. We tried the jib sail but had no luck with the serpentine turns and little wind. The good news is that we arrived before lunch, and I believe that's a first.

St Augustine is a beautiful Spanish-flavored city. We dinghied into the marina, and for $7, we can tie up and use the showers which we will enjoy tomorrow. Today, it was just nice to walk around the town and pick up some odds and ends.

Back on the boat, we dined on deck, and it felt like we were in Disney World with all the twinkling Christmas lights in the distance. It was quite enchanting.

December 1, 1998

It was time to take advantage of those showers, and so we did. We returned to *Perpetual* fresh and clean to find that the anchor had fouled under the keel, but with the kind assistance of a fellow boater, we were able to free it. The fellow boater then recognized the name *Perpetual* and announced that we were the boat that radioed them warning of the shoals out of the infamous Elliot Cut as they went aground in spite of our warning, and then we did too. It was fun reliving that day, knowing that neither boat was harmed and we all made it to Florida in spite of ourselves.

We decided we needed to see more of St Augustine, so we dinghied in, found a sweet cafe for lunch, and ambled around the waterfront.

The Christmas spirit is with us as we make our way to North Palm Beach. It's so exciting to know that we'll be seeing our family in less than three weeks.

December 2, 1998

We left St. Augustine with some regret, but with 200 miles to go, we were on purpose to make North Palm Beach in two weeks. Our destination today was an anchorage thirty miles south by a cement factory.

Our first event of the day was retrieving Ann's hat, which blew off as we were sailing. It was good practice for a man overboard drill. It was with great precision that I turned the boat, and Ann scooped up the hat. We were quite pleased with our success. Later, however, Ann was at the helm when we hit bottom in an area where the Waterway Guide reported extreme shoaling. I was the navigator and hadn't read those details until after the fact. Thank God we were off after a few minutes. Reading ahead was my lesson for the day.

We found the anchorage with two other boats present, a small basin just as had been described, not particularly picturesque but functional.

December 3, 1998

Another day of scrupulously following the charts and, of course, reading ahead, however, in the northern channel of the Ponce de Leon Inlet, keeping red to the right as required, we hit bottom. It took the wake of a passing boat to luckily get us off, and again, how grateful we were and are to this community who are always around to help.

We found an anchorage in a creek off the inlet, and what a magnificent spot. We watched the full moon rise in the eastern sky and the sun set in the west with the pinkest sky all around. It felt miraculous, perhaps because it is.

December 4, 1998

Our original plan was to leave for Titusville today. We had made reservations at the Kennedy Point Yacht Club, but when we awoke at seven, we thought, why don't we stay another day and explore the beach? We packed a lunch and dinghied into a pretty secluded beach and read, played Scrabble, and watched dolphins. This is a wonderful life, and we are so thoroughly enjoying ourselves. I sometimes wonder if I'll ever be able to fully return to life on land.

December 5, 1998

It was hard leaving Rockhouse Creek, but onto our next adventure.

We traveled some forty miles today and are proud to say we did not hit the ground once, not without some hair-standing moments, however. We found Kennedy Point Yacht Club with its six-foot channel entrance and proceeded cautiously with success.

We had seen Captain Perry and his wife Joann in St Augustine, and they thought they would meet us here since their condo is nearby; however, the dock master informed us that they had called and would be delayed until Sunday. Later on, while doing the laundry, Joann's family arrived and introduced themselves, saying Perry had called and wanted them to offer his car so we could shop. How considerate and kind. Two weeks ago, we hadn't even met Captain Perry. We thanked them for the offer, but we were pretty tired and decided to walk next door to the Holiday Inn for a hamburger. Shopping could wait.

December 6, 1998

It seems there are a lot of people who know each other at this marina, and it has quite a friendly atmosphere with boats all decked out with Christmas lights. A beautiful red-hull sailboat named *Keno* stood out, and we quickly made our acquaintance with the owners, Mary and Jim. They are leaving for Puerto Rico in a couple of days and bringing their cat, Nonsense. Mary has crossed the Atlantic three times and seems like a very accomplished sailor. I so enjoy hearing other sailors tell their stories of life at sea. It's never boring.

That afternoon, Perry and Joann arrived, and we made a plan to meet tomorrow for dinner as they still had house guests.

December 7, 1998

Had a wonderful relaxing day playing tennis and hanging out by the pool. Erin, a cute ten-year-old who has lived on a boat since she was ten months old, became fast friends with us, especially with Ann, who frolicked in the pool for hours.

Ann was a tad tired but perked up when Perry and Joann arrived to take us to the famous Dixie Crossroads, which is renowned for its seafood and rock shrimp, which I had to try—very tasty. It was fun listening to their various adventures as they told us about living in Saudi Arabia, sailing the Greek Islands, and living in Centerport, New York, before retiring to Florida. Such a small world as I presently have a house in Centerport, New York.

What a delightful evening.

December 8, 1998

It's farewell time at the marina. Said goodbye to Perry and Joann with hopes we could see them on our return home. *Keno*, the red-hulled sailboat, has also left, and now it was time for *Perpetual* to get going.

We decided to travel only fifteen miles today since we didn't get started till early afternoon. We anchored with a group of other boats just north of Cocoa, Florida. According to our trusted Waterway Guide, the town of Cocoa sounds interesting, so we'll layover for a day of exploration.

December 9, 1998

Haven't been sleeping well because of those damn hot flashes and wound up taking a couple of Benadryl last night and now feel a bit drugged this morning. I am glad we had decided to have a play day in Cocoa.

We dinghied into the marina and were informed we could tie up at the little sandy beach.

To our delight, we found a gem of a town with plenty of gift shops and nice restaurants. Here we were walking around in shorts, with Christmas music playing, and it was not hard to get used to. We found a great store called The Piano Man, where we bought a piano tie for my brother and a music box doll playing the violin for his partner Andy. Time for lunch, and we dined in a sweet cafe.

Ann had to call The Registry of Motor Vehicles about her so-to-be-expired license and had some momentary feelings of pure frustration as she lost money on the pay phone and made no progress in connecting with the right office. It was sort of a reminder of what life used to be like on land when, at least a few times a week, something similar occurred.

It was with great pleasure that we hopped into the dinghy and headed back to *Perpetual,* where life is so much more peaceful and simple, at least most of the time.

December 10, 1998

Two weeks from today is Christmas Eve, and all of the kids should have arrived by then. Ann called to reserve a car as we will be making lots of airport trips.

We are heading into the last few days of this trek and feeling pretty excited and always grateful for experiencing such an adventure as we pick up the anchor and head off to a new destination. Today, we will go about twenty-five miles, and it's another beautiful day. In fact, since we began our trip in August, we have had only a handful of rainy days.

The terrain of Florida is strikingly different from the Lowcountry of South Carolina; there are no more marshes and wetlands, and the surrounding shores are now heavily treed with modern homes and occasional high-rise condos and hotels.

The ICW was wide today, but the channel was still pretty narrow, which we scrupulously followed. The wind was blowing at 5 to 10, so we hoisted both sails, turned off the engine, and enjoyed two hours of pure sailing, gliding through the water with the only sound of "shlop, shlop" as the water smacked against the dinghy. I never get tired of this. I don't think I could ever own a trawler.

Another beautiful anchorage, a bit shallow, but no tidal change, so we should be ok. Sitting here right now in the absolute quiet except for the "shlop, shlop" of the dinghy and having just taken marvelous cockpit showers, watching another breathtaking sunset, life could not get any better than this. I know I say that a lot, but it's so true.

December 11, 1998

Awakened to a glorious sunrise and began our trek to Vero Beach. The trip was quite scenic, with some exquisite homes on the shoreline. We passed the famous Jones Fruit Dock, where boaters can tie up and buy fruit. It's been in existence for many years, but we, however, didn't stop.

Arrived in Vero Beach just in time for lunch but first stopped at the fuel dock and replenished the diesel and water. We were then assigned to a mooring. It had been described in our guide that we might have to fender up with other boats if necessary, but tonight, we would have a mooring all to ourselves. If we wanted showers, it would be $1.00 a piece, such a deal! We picked up our mooring and decided to take a dinghy ride up the canal for some needed items, wine being one of them. About a mile up, we tied to a dock and found a lovely little shopping area with a great wine store and market. On the way back, we spotted the red hull *Keno* and spoke with Jim and Mary, who told us that the weather hadn't been good for going offshore, so they were sitting in a spell with lots of other boats. Apparently, those going through the Gulf Stream need a southerly wind, or it can be extremely dangerous. We found out later that many boats were laid up waiting here and also anywhere near Lake Worth, awaiting the right wind. The rumor was that, as a result, the anchorages were packed. We had a moment of concern since we would be anchoring after leaving here. Can't think about that now; it's dinner time.

December 12, 1998

Didn't feel that great today, so I took it slow and just putzed around the boat. We thought we might have a cooler leak, so we took up the floor and dried it out. Later, we took the dinghy into the marina and luxuriated in those $1.00 showers. It was so good. On the way back to the boat, a dolphin leaped out of the water right next to us. What a moment!

We now have a neighbor on a small Catamaran who single-handed his boat from New Hampshire. We introduced ourselves and made some small talk. I hate to sound snobby, but it feels a little too intimate with someone you don't know in such close proximity, especially a man. Oh well, we shall see. Cest la vie sur la bateau *Perpetual*. This is life aboard *Perpetual*.

I'm beginning to feel better as I enjoyed a Coke during cocktail hour and listened to Christmas music.

December 13, 1998

Well, the good news is that nothing untoward happened last night, and our neighbor is leaving today. We decided to stay an extra day as a cold front is coming in today with threats of thunderstorms.

Dinghied into the marina to do a wash and wound up finally writing Christmas cards dressed in shorts and tee shirts.

We'll be off in the morning for the last two days of the journey for 1998. It's hard to believe.

December 14, 1998

The cold front arrived last night, and we awoke in a very chilly cabin; so much for mocking hot weather at Christmas time. It feels like New York weather, with the wind howling at 20.

Out on the waterway, it was rather cloudy, but since the wind was behind us, we pulled out the genoa and ran downwind. It was a glorious reminder of *Perpetual's* maiden voyage around Long Island Sound in May of 1997, the cool stiff breeze and actual white caps with a following sea. In truth, we had never seen the ICW so churned up, and it felt beautifully exhilarating. We were having a grand ole time until we arrived at the Crossroads of the St Lucie Inlet. Ann was navigating and warned me that it would be tricky. It was here the ICW, the Okeechobee Waterway, and the Indian River meet. The ICW markers go two ways, and the sea buoys lead you out into the ocean. So, of course, the captain and the navigator had different opinions regarding the ICW buoys, and before committing to either, thank the heavens, I had the presence of mind to turn around and get my bearings. In doing so, I realized my navigator was right, and had I taken the buoy to starboard, we would have been aground. I quickly apologized and avoided mutiny on the high seas.

We anchored in a place called Manatee Pocket, a secluded hurricane hole, and fixed a great dinner of leftovers. We had an awesome game of Scrabble where I scored a forty-seven-point word and still lost, but I am getting much better, I must say.

December 15, 1998

The Bruce anchor we bought in North Carolina is fabulous. We had anchored in only five and a half feet of water, and it held great.

We needed a few items, so we decided to dinghy ashore and check out Port Salerno. Found the post office, mailed our Christmas cards and gifts, and treated ourselves to breakfast at a cafe nearby.

The Journey of *Perpetual*

The Chapman School of Seamanship is located in Port Salerno, and as we were eating breakfast, we could overhear the students discussing navigation questions since they would be taking the exam that afternoon. There were also lots of fishermen talking about the catch of the day and the change in weather. The sun was shining as we left, and we were well-layered for basically our last sail for 1998.

Back on *Perpetual* and ready to depart, little did we know that today would present some major challenges. As we entered the Crossroads again, we thought we were now pretty savvy in our navigation and were feeling rather confident until we saw a dredging operation clearly blocking our access to the green buoy. Earlier in town, we had spoken to a Sea Tow captain who advised us of the extreme shoals and, when we saw the barge and tug, that we should hug the eastern shore. We did not see that possibility and tried hugging close to the barge, and of course, we went aground. The crane was operating right next to us, so Ann radioed the tug, who told us he had been trying to contact us to warn us to come around to the other side. Praise God, we rocked off, avoiding the crane, and found better water. Ann was now on the helm, and we had barely caught our breath when another huge barge—and I mean the largest I had ever seen—was attempting to share the channel with *Perpetual*. Oh my!!! We thought we left those monsters in the Chesapeake, and here they are on the Gold Coast. The good news is it was close, but no ground touching this time or hitting the barge, again another prayer of thanks.

The Gold Coast, by the way, began as we entered southern Florida at the Intracoastal mile 1,000. The shoreline is lush with vegetation and luxurious homes, and the visual became a welcome distraction from the momentary terror we were periodically experiencing.

As we were approaching the Jupiter Highway Bridge, I radioed the bridge to request an opening, and the reply was there was no such bridge. But there before my eyes was a bridge that our guide said was the Jupiter Highway Bridge. It wasn't until we described what buoy we were at that it finally opened. We still had five more bascule bridges to contend with, and we hoped this was just a fluke from a bored bridge tender wanting to play a trick. Happy to say it was, as we pulled into a small canal that felt like a cul-de-sac in development, with homes grouped together and boats tied to pilings instead of cars in driveways.

December 16, 1998

We had approximately one and a half miles to go where we would park *Perpetual* in a marina for the next three weeks. We had rented a house way back last winter before we left to accommodate everyone.

It was quite windy, and we had to deal with our last bridge. We were right on time for the opening and radioed the bridge tender, who told us to bring her right up to the bridge, which we did. Another sailboat was also waiting, and the current was pretty stiff. The bridge tender radioed that he was having trouble with the opening, so we turned around and waited patiently, far enough away from the bridge. It was only about ten minutes, and it finally opened, and we found Old Port Marina in North Palm Beach.

We had truly made it after four months, and it almost felt anticlimactic. It was now time to pick up our rental car at the airport and call our friend Iris, who we would be staying with until we took over our house.

Living on the water certainly has its demands, but for the most part, we had become pretty comfortable with them. It was now time to test our land skills, and we felt a bit nervous. Isn't life amazing?

January 10, 1999

At this very moment, we are anchored right outside St Lucie Inlet, and after over three weeks of being on land, it feels wonderful to return to our lives at sea. The candles are aglow again, and pine cone punks permeate a sweet scent throughout the cabin. It's a good time to write about our time in Palm Beach.

The last three weeks, though, were magnificent, and as I look back on our Christmas in Palm Beach. I can only feel thankful for all the joy, laughter, and closeness that I know everyone experienced.

The house was perfect and provided the space for everyone to mingle or just relax. The pool and patio were where we mostly hung out, playing volleyball or intense Scrabble and hilarious Guesstures games. Then, there was frenetic furniture moving in the living room to accommodate a beautiful eight-foot Christmas tree. The dining room was where a perplexing puzzle turned into a beautiful pink and purple butterfly, completed at 1 a.m. Christmas morning. I can't forget to mention the piano playing on the beautiful white baby grand along with drumming, guitar strumming, and listening to the famous Boys Choir over and over and over again. The state-of-the-art kitchen, overlooking the ICW, was where everyone just took turns creating delicious cuisine. The four private bedrooms, plus a loft, provided absolute comatose slumber where everyone regained some energy to start all over again.

We were so excited to see everyone. Erin, Ann's daughter, and Chris, her partner, arrived first from California. We hadn't even moved into the house yet, so they stayed on the boat for two nights while we stayed with our friend Iris. It was then to Miami, where Jordan arrived from India. Next were Patrick, my son, and his wife, Kris, who arrived in Fort Lauderdale from Arizona, followed by my daughter Lisa and her husband Mike, who landed in Palm Beach from New York. Every flight was amazingly on time, which in itself was miraculous just days before Christmas.

All were together by Christmas Eve, and we had a delicious dinner where conversation flowed nonstop. Christmas morning, in front of the tree, I found everyone receiving their Secret Santa gifts as the aroma of Turkey permeated the house. The temperature was seventy-five degrees and perfect for volleyball in the pool.

Marie and Carol arrived from New Jersey the next night. Ann's sister Mary, who lives in Florida, drove over for a visit with her young grandchildren Dillon and Chase, who became fast friends with Lisa and Erin as they frolicked wildly in the pool. Mike's family, who was visiting Florida, stopped by the same day as our New York friends Johanna and Cindy, followed by Iris and her friend Trudy. It was quite an eclectic impromptu gathering with more pool volleyball for those who wished and lots of food and drinks. Hitting our waterbed that night was with great intention, to say the least.

All the kids were gone by New Year's Eve, and then Tommy, Ann's brother, and his partner, Sara, arrived full of total energy and laughter. Ann and I could barely stand up but managed to rally in the contagious spirit with Marie and Carol, Marilyn and Maryann, who arrived from Boca and spent a memorable New Year's Eve cooking and eating magnificent steaks along with Tommy's famous twice-baked potatoes. As midnight approached, it was time for a Happy Birthday to Ann as we brought in 1999 and her 55th birthday.

The day we moved out of the house, it rained thirty-one inches. Parts of Palm Beach were flooded. Since the dinghy was full of water and the waterway was blowing hard, we decided to wait a day to bring the dinghy back to the boat.

We were now off to stay with Iris again for a few days, who could not have been kinder and more accommodating even though she was in the middle of packing for her own move and had another house guest, Harriet, from New York. Harriet was a bit uptight since she was buying a condo and looking for a job, but after a couple of days with us, she managed to lighten up a bit. We even got her to hit some tennis balls.

My brother Tom was visiting Florida with his friend Sydney and met up with us for a very quick lunch as we were now moving back aboard *Perpetual,* which necessitated a major provisioning from Publix.

As much as we had such a great time with all our family and friends, we are currently relishing the peace, quiet, and simplicity of life aboard *Perpetual,* currently anchored in Peck Lake.

LAKE OKEECHOBEE TO
THE WEST COAST OF FLORIDA

January 11, 1999

Woke up to a cold, windy morning and found our depth sounder reading three and a half feet. *Perpetual* had found the shoal, and we were aground. It was with some difficulty that Ann managed to free the anchor as I gunned the engine, and alas, we were off. Our Plan was to cross Lake Okeechobee, the body of water that would ultimately take us to the West Coast of Florida. Joan and Evie, our friends from New York, have invited us to spend a few days with them at a condo they rented in Bradenton Beach, Florida.

As we approached the St Lucie Inlet, the winds were blowing 25 knots. We hadn't done this in a while, and it felt challenging, to say the least. Again, the Crossroads was our nemesis, but we negotiated the buoys correctly into the St Lucie River and did quite well until a bascule bridge appeared that we hadn't planned on. Sometimes, these bridges have only scheduled openings. Ann quickly hurried down below to radio for an opening. She didn't even know the name of the bridge as it wasn't mentioned in our trusty guide. It quickly opened, and it was now time to let in the momentary terror that we hadn't had time to experience. Yes, we were back on the water.

Today's destination was Indiantown Marina, where sailboats with large masts can have them unstepped to negotiate the forty-nine-foot railroad bridge, or if you just need a couple of feet of clearance, you can have fifty-five-gallon drums filled with water strapped to the side of your boat to tip it enough. The latter sounded dicey to me. I knew our mast was forty-five feet, but I was feeling a bit tentative and wanted some reassurance. Amazingly, as we were docking the boat, a woman came over and said she also had a Pearson 28 and pointed to it. Yes, the mast is forty-five feet; we would make it with four feet of clearance.

They had just come through and were heading east. There are times like this I believe we are being guided by forces bigger than ourselves.

January 12-16, 1999

It's time to recall our journey across the Okeechobee.

After leaving Indiantown Marina, it was time to go under that infamous railroad bridge. We proceeded slowly with some trepidation. Even though we had gotten reassurance, It truly did not look like we had four feet of clearance, but we did

The dreaded Port Mayaca railroad bridge

All in all, the rest of the trip went fairly well. The weather cooperated, especially crossing Lake Okeechobee itself, which can be extremely dangerous in very windy weather as it is quite shallow, and the waves can be erratic and unforgiving. We were fortunate to have a calm wind and managed to sail across this expansive body of water, the largest freshwater lake in Florida.

We had to do seven locks in total. That in itself was sometimes complicated, as we got scolded once by the lock master for not doing things correctly. From there, we got better.

From Indiantown, we stopped at Clewiston, which was not very interesting, although the marina was nice. Then, on to La Belle, where we pulled into a free town dock with a few other boats and learned how to drop a stern anchor. However, the next day, retrieving it became very difficult, especially because we were not aligned about the plan of departure and should have gotten some assistance with the anchor. So much for hindsight. It was in strong silence that we made the eight-hour trek into Fort Myers and later began a two-hour-long process to clear the air. I'm happy to say the Captain and Navigator are back to normal after learning some valuable lessons.

We are staying at a marina that our new friends Bob and Colleen recommended. It had just been built; however, the showers and laundry facilities had not been completed, and that's what we desperately needed. When we told the dockmaster that we were leaving because of this, he gave us permission to use the facilities in the model condo, which more than satisfied our needs.

We just heard from Marie and Carol that Ann's cat Fletcher has died. They had kindly volunteered to take Fletcher while we were on our trip. I was never a cat person till I met Fletcher, and he won me over, big time. We are both feeling very sad but are relieved he didn't suffer. He had just eaten, walked into the living room, and keeled over.

Heading North on the West Coast of Florida

January 17, 1999

We met Colleen and Bob last evening for dinner at a lovely restaurant. We enjoyed good food and catching up, as we last saw them at the Alligator Pungo River. They have been in Fort Myers, staying at an elegant marina complex for the past two months. They proposed a plan to anchor out with us for a few days as we travel north to Bradenton Beach, so we made a plan to rendezvous at their marina today and take off on Monday.

It was a short trip to this fancy Gulf Harbor Marina, and we arrived early to take full advantage of all its perks. The weather was beautiful, and we spent the day in and out of the pool and or Jacuzzi and then to the club tennis courts, followed by gorgeous warm showers. Colleen took us shopping, which we desperately needed to do, and then prepared an awesome dinner as we made plans for our anchoring venture.

January 18, 1999

Today would be quite easy as our destination was Ding Darling National Wildlife Refuge off Sanibel Island. We would have to pay strict attention to the buoys as the water is very "skinny," but we are very used to that by now.

Colleen and Bob had already anchored, and all we had to do was raft up with them. After rafting up, we dinghied around the refuge but never made it to shore as the area is surrounded by mangroves where an abundance of various birds and maybe even some alligators can be found. That's one scary thought! I forgot to mention that Colleen and Bob have a tiny Yorkshire Terrier named Moose and have become very astute at managing the swampy terrain where Moose does his business. Thankfully, there have been no alligator sightings. On the way back to our boats, we spotted a school of Dolphins that we followed. What a spectacular way to spend an afternoon and get rid of reptile thoughts.

Back on *Perpetual*, we got busy preparing dinner as it was our turn to host. Ann made her delicious potato salad, corn on the cob, and barbecued steaks. It was very cozy in our tiny cabin, and the ambiance, with the candlelight and music, was just right.

This Martin Luther King Holiday will always be remembered.

January 19, 1999

Another easy day of sailing, eight miles to Tween Water Marina on Captiva Island. This time, however, Colleen and Bob's anchoring efforts proved unsuccessful as they went aground briefly. Meanwhile, we stopped for fuel at the marina, not knowing their distress but finding out within moments as they barreled in behind us. Their decision was not to anchor and stay at the marina. After talking with the dock master, we decided to anchor since he gave us specific instructions on how to avoid the sandbar.

After setting anchor, the day was still young, so we were off in our dinghy to shore. There, across a two-lane road, was the beautiful turquoise Gulf of Mexico, where we parked and played Scrabble, followed by a delicious dinner aboard *Long Shot,* where we all watched this incredible fog roll in. Returning to *Perpetual* was no easy feat, but thankfully, we found her, and by the way, so did the sandbar. Grounded and at anchor, yuck, we will deal with it tomorrow.

January 20, 1999

Woke up to absolute pea soup fog. We could barely see the boat next to us. After a cup of coffee, I decided to brave it and dinghy into the dock, knowing the general direction. I found Colleen and Bob, and we talked about alternate plans. It was unanimous that we were staying another day, a very wise move.

Back on *Perpetual,* which was no longer aground, we reset the anchor. The visibility was definitely better on land, so we returned to the marina and found a tennis court to get some exercise. It was our turn to cook dinner, so Ann prepared a beef stroganoff that was a big hit as we sat safely aboard *Perpetual,* no longer aground on a foggy warm evening in the middle of January. What a difference a day makes.

January 21, 1999

The weather report was predicting heavy winds coming in by Saturday, so we were all a bit concerned about our next destination. The good news though was that the sky was blue and the visibility crystal clear. We all decided to anchor together another night in Cayo Costa, a short run that would put us a few miles north toward our destination, Bradenton Beach.

We were all so pleasantly surprised to find a beautiful State Park off the anchorage. After rafting up with *Long Shot*, Colleen, Ann, and I dinghied in and walked a beautiful tree-lined path to the nine miles of the pristine uninhabited Gulf beach, where we played Scrabble, marveling about our surrounding beauty.

That night, we feasted on board *Long Shot*, enjoying our last evening together. Tomorrow, they will be returning to Gulf Harbor Marina as we proceed north to Bradenton Beach.

January 22, 1999

Woke up early so we could leave our anchorage, as the entrance had only five to six feet of water at high tide. Bob and Colleen had already dinghied into shore to walk Moose. All of a sudden, I saw them waving to me to come, so I jumped in the dinghy, wondering if they needed help. Sure enough, their outbound had died, and they had forgotten to take the oars. They had actually been yelling for a while. Safely back on board, we bid our farewells with hopes of connecting again either on our return trip from Bradenton or back in the Chesapeake.

The wind was blowing pretty hard, but fortunately, behind us, so we could run downwind and be in Sarasota by afternoon.

We pulled into Marina Jack and were tied to a dock where, unfortunately, next to us was a large Paddle Boat that was also a restaurant. Between the emitting food odors and choppy waters, we both were having some stomach issues. Hopefully, we will find another spot tomorrow.

January 23, 1999

Feeling better this morning, we decided to do laundry and prepare for the big storm that was supposedly coming later today. We moved to another slip right off the park and delighted in the aroma of pending rain rather than garlic and fish.

The wind was howling, and the amazing lightning was flashing in the sky, but no thunder, so weird and a little scary. After talking with my son Pat, in Arizona, who told me this occurs frequently there and to just stay safe and try and enjoy the sights, which we ultimately did.

Down below in our cozy cabin, as I read my entry for the day to Ann, she promptly reminded me that I had forgotten about our hair dye episode in Sarasota. So here it is.

We purchased the dye at a shop in downtown Sarasota. At first, I got the same color as Ann but then decided to change to a golden brown. There we were, in the bathroom of Marina Jack's, as people meandered to and fro, glancing at two scary sights sitting on the floor, waiting for the time to pass as the dye did its magic. Ann's magic looked great. Mine, however, was unmagical as the color turned to auburn red as I looked in the mirror and wondered who was staring back.

January 24, 1999

Today our plan was to be in Bradenton Beach by afternoon. Our friends Evie and Joan had rented a place where some other friends from New York were also arriving to spend a couple of weeks in paradise.

Spent at least an hour trying to get out of our slip. The winds were gusting up to 20 knots and pushing us back into the slip. It was with great patience and brute strength that we finally got free.

Meanwhile, out in the bay, it was blowing pretty hard, and as we waited for the bridge to open, we contemplated the prudence of our actions. It was 2:30, and we had the Sarasota Bay to contend with. Was it worth it?? No, became the resounding answer, and we returned to Sarasota, anchored, and called Evie and Joan to tell them we would hopefully be with them by the next afternoon.

It was time to have an early Sunday dinner and read the NY Times.

January 25, 1999

We left our protected anchorage and once again attempted our short passage to Bradenton Beach. What a difference a day makes. The bay was flat, and the winds were about five to ten.

We were motoring with the jib when we heard a loud slapping sound. Upon inspection, one of the belts had frayed a bit. We decided to turn the engine off and use it only when necessary. We sailed most of the way, but turning into Anna Maria Sound, the wind was in our faces. We turned the engine on, and thankfully, it worked fine. What a beautiful sight to behold. Our friends Evie, Joan, Aline, Jean, and their friend Darline all frantically waved to us from the dock as we safely brought *Perpetual* to a halt. What an awesome welcome we received.

A mechanic will be replacing the worn belt tomorrow.

We will now be spending a whole two weeks with everyone. Let the party begin!

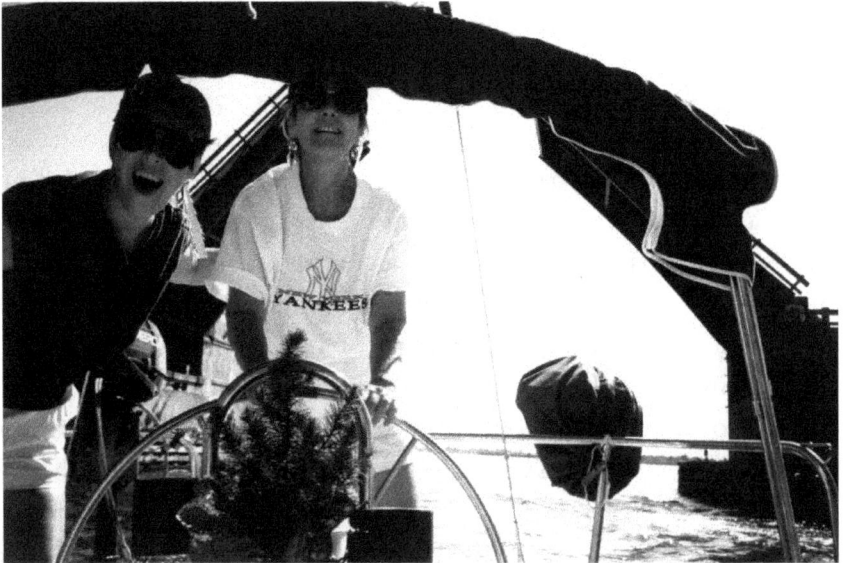

Tampa Bay

February 7, 1999

What an incredible two weeks we had. Evie and Joan's place had what I call a "Riverhead quality." They have a small cabin in Riverhead, Long Island, where when you are there, you feel right at home, and now we were not only right at home but also right on the beach, just steps away from the gorgeous Gulf. The magnificent sunsets, the rhythmic pounding of the surf that lulled us to sleep at night, and lots of laughter, who could want anything more?

Jean and Aline were eager to go for a sail, and it was delightful to find deep water in the beautiful Tampa Bay, where Aline learned the lingo to radio the bridge for an opening while Jean took the helm.

We'll never forget playing miniature golf and Aline's two holes-in-one as she peed in her pants from the excitement and laughter. Then, on to the "all you can eat pizza" night, where everyone sampled many different kinds of pizza, including pineapple, and miraculously no one got sick.

Everyone loved walking down the beach to have breakfast at the Waffle House, where we enjoyed watching Joan eat her waffles topped with mounds of whipped cream and strawberries.

We are so grateful for Evie's countless taxiing, especially for finding a West Marine where we were able to purchase a GPS and, of course, lest I forget, driving us and waiting for hours in the Blake Hospital ER where Ann had part of a Q-tip removed from her ear.

Ann's sister Mary and husband Fred drove down from Palm Harbor for an enjoyable lunch, and their son Chuck arrived the next day to give us some valuable instructions on using our newly acquired GPS. We went out for a sail and marveled at this new technology.

Tomorrow, we move back on board *Perpetual* and start heading south.

Heading south on the west coast of Florida

February 8, 1999

After shedding some tears when Evie dropped us off, we left Bradenton and headed back to Sarasota. It was a great two weeks, but *Perpetual* is our home for now, and it feels so good to be back on the water.

Our long-range plan is to sail the gulf, go to Key West, and come back up the East Coast.

The short-run back to Sarasota was uneventful, and we returned to the same anchorage we left two weeks ago. We were the only boat but were quickly joined by another boat whose owner was having trouble anchoring. We certainly know that frustration as my trusty navigator tried offering some suggestions.

February 9, 1999

Woke up to some fog that quickly burned off. After our ritual morning coffee, we were off to Venice. There were no gondolas, but they did have a free dock. We arrived early to find a spot on the dock, and our boat neighbor from last night took our line. He invited us to have some leftover pizza, but we declined since we were saving our appetites for lunch in town.

It was time to explore Venice via bike. We quickly found the Crow's Nest, where we had the most delicious seafood chowder as we sat overlooking the Venice Inlet that leads to the Gulf. There was a rock jetty going out to the sea where lots of people were fishing or just taking in the view. On to the downtown area, we spotted tennis courts, which were open to the public. We'll be back, but for now, on to the post office to send Valentines to the kids.

I returned to watch tennis, and Ann went to the bank. Meanwhile, a man pulled up in a car and started chatting. He was from Oyster Bay, New York, a town not far from where I used to live. We had a friendly chat, and I probably gave him more info than was necessary, as evidenced by his turning up at the dock the next day. He wanted to show us around town. We thanked him and said we were just off to play tennis. He then reported he had just passed by the courts, and they were packed; we would never get to play.

"We'll take our chances; we need the exercise," Ann replied.

"I'll meet you there." This seemed a little Pushy with a capital P.

We arrived at the courts and signed up. We would be paired with two men for mixed doubles. Jack sat in his car, finally got the point, and said goodbye as we waved. We played for over an hour and had great rallies. We then went for haircuts and wound up at the beach and didn't see Jack again.

SAILING THE BEAUTIFUL
GULF OF MEXICO

February 11, 1999

Wow, we are currently sailing in the Gulf of Mexico, heading for Boca Grande. What a magnificent moment this is. Our first time venturing out into the Gulf of Mexico with a gentle breeze of 8-10 knots. The sails are full, the turquoise water is calm, and every so often, a dolphin pokes out of the water. We are attempting to use our newly purchased GPS as my navigator just commented, "I like this little thing." Having made the journey up to now, with no such instrumentation, this is a God-send.

The sail in itself was fair since we were beating pretty close to the wind and wanted to stay on the compass course, so we motored a good part of the way following the GPS, which brought us to the buoy that would lead us into the Boca Grande Inlet.

Our plan was to anchor in what the Waterway Guide described as a "bayou and to anchor Mediterranean style, bow anchor in the water and stern line tied to the mangrove." It sounded pretty dicey since we had no idea what a bayou was and absolutely no sense of Mediterranean-style anchoring. When we rounded the corner where the gorgeous, pristine golf course lay separated from the water by the mangroves, we found at least twelve boats all lined up and anchored as previously described. After setting our bow anchor and backing in, Ann hopped into the dinghy, line in hand, and tied the stern to the tree; pretty formidable! I have to admit we were pretty pleased with ourselves and declared it was Miller Time as we shared a Corona. I am slowly beginning to understand what the saying "just do it" means. Thinking about something can sometimes cause more angst than the task itself.

We decided since a storm was approaching, we'd stay in this protected bayou for a few days and explore the island. It's so nice not to have a schedule.

February 12, 1999

It's hard to believe a storm is coming as presently there are beautiful blue skies and light, balmy breezes.

It was time to explore Gasparilla Island, so out came the bikes lowered carefully into the dinghy, and we were off. Only a short ride to a lovely dock, and we were now on this most enchanting island, very upscale, to say the least, as we noted the real estate prices. The village is charming, with lots of shops, a fully stocked market, and nice restaurants. The homes have an old look and, I'm sure, pretty pricey. We found the public tennis courts and will definitely take advantage of them after visiting a private tennis club where a tournament was currently occurring. And since I needed some tennis balls, I paid the requisite $5.00 and tried not to look so shocked about the price. People there seemed a wee bit stuffy.

We were curious to see what people do for health care, living on this beautiful island, so off we went to the state-of-the-art health clinic. The woman at the front desk was less than friendly as I asked some basic questions. I did find out that they do not take insurance. So glad we have no health issues presently.

We decided to return to our anchorage, where the people there are more down to earth, and enjoyed a nice evening, waiting for the storm while eating dinner topside and gazing at the most beautiful star-covered sky.

February 13, 1999

One thing I must say is that NOAA weather reports are pretty much on target. Our big blue comforter came to the rescue as the temperature dropped and the winds were howling in the wee hours of the morning. It was hard to leave our cozy v-berth, but we were anxious to see how the stern line held on the mangrove.

Up on deck, we were thrilled to see the line had held pretty well. It felt like a fall morning in New York as we layered up and planned our day over some hot coffee. It's amazing how every day is like Saturday when you are not working, and we never seem to tire of this lifestyle with its new adventures unfolding daily. It may be cold, but the sun is shining, and just sitting here watching all the bird life in the mangroves is spectacular: blue herons, Great Egrets, and my favorite of all, Pelicans. I know life will never be the same.

We dinghied into the dock where we had left our bikes locked like all the other boaters. We decided to take a five-mile bike trip to the north end of the island. What an invigorating ride with the cold wind on our faces; we were very happy to be wearing jeans and sweaters. The bike trails were super and so nice not to contend with cars, just occasional golf carts. We found a sweet little cafe at Uncle Henry's Marina and had a delicious bowl of fish chowder while watching the cheerleading finals on their very prominent TV. On the return trip, we stopped at an open-air art festival. We were now back in shorts. Florida weather, I love it!!

Back on *Perpetual*, we played a fierce game of Scrabble, where I almost won.

February 14, 1999

Happy Valentine's Day, and happy birthday to my brother Billy.

Another picture-perfect day. It definitely was a tennis day, and we played twice, with lunch in between. We took a bike ride to the beach, where the surf was very rough, and we were quite happy not to be sailing out there today. We read the NY Times, which was full of info regarding Clinton's acquittal. Since we began our trip, this story has followed us down the waterway, and now it's over. It sparked some good debates between Ann and me as the whole debacle unfolded, but now that it's done, we're both glad.

Back on *Perpetual*, we had a wonderful romantic dinner of grilled steak and the works, topped off with some Bordeaux wine, as we again marveled at our surrounding beauty. We will never forget Valentine's Day 1999.

February 15, 1999

It's hard to leave such a precious spot, but it was time to move on. Ann hopped into the dinghy, untied the stern line from the mangrove, and hurriedly climbed back on board to pull up the anchor as I steered forward, and we were free. As we turned out of the bayou, we noted white caps and, for a moment, contemplated returning to our safe haven; however, by afternoon, the wind let up, and we were making a great time to Sanibel Island, so we thought. As we approached the bridge, Ann radioed to request an opening, but no response. Then we noticed there was no little house where the bridge tender sat, and in fact, it was a fixed bridge; the opening bridge would be another one and a half hours later. Oops! My navigator had misjudged.

We were happy to pull into the Sanibel Marina, where we did tons of laundry.

February 16, 1999

Off on our bikes to explore the island. We found it to be very built up and extremely crowded. We had forgotten that this was school vacation week, and this is a popular destination since it's accessible by car. Luckily for us, the bike paths were great, but the beach was packed, and it was unbearably hot, over ninety degrees, so we found a nice cafe for lunch, followed by an air-conditioned movie, *Shakespeare in Love,* and had a glorious day.

February 17, 1999

We are now sitting at anchor at Fort Myers Beach after an exhausting but very productive day.

We had a lot of boat-keeping chores to do before we left, including washing the anchor rode, hanging the Danforth anchor back on the bow just in case we needed two anchors, arranging the lines in the anchor well so we don't have a tangled mess, cleaning the dinghy, scrubbing the deck and basically getting things in order down below.

After showering, we were off into the Gulf, where the wind was honking, and the seas were at least three feet. The jib pulled us over to Ft Myers beach on a course of eighty-five degrees to green buoy #1. We pulled in the jib and entered a well-marked channel to find Moss Marine, where we were finally able to pump out the holding tank and fill up on diesel. It feels good to be empty and yet full, I declared to Ann, and we both laughed.

February 18, 1999

The Waterway Guide describes Fort Myers Beach as a place for many liveaboards. The currents are very strong, and two anchors may be in order. We seem to be holding well with one, so off to do some shopping via dinghy. It was convenient, with the supermarket, wine store, and drugstore all in the same vicinity, as well as the beach across the street, where we parked for a short time after shopping.

Back on board *Perpetual*, Ann had just finished her shower, and I was in the middle of mine when I heard a strange voice as Ann remarked, "We're looking mighty close." Our anchor had slipped. Our stern was right into the bow of another sailboat, and the Captain was worried that his anchor line would get stuck on our rudder. Thankfully, it didn't, as he paid out more line and gilded back. We however had to reset our anchor, but because of the strong current, it was taut against the hull, and we couldn't free it. Our new neighbor arrived by kayak and helped us pull the line. There on our chain was a piece of old rusted chain and some cloth, perhaps the culprit. After resetting the anchor, we offered Don a beer for his assistance, which he accepted. Then, he sat and chatted for a short while. We were glad he didn't prolong his stay. He seemed harmless, but there is an uneasy feeling when we meet a man traveling solo. You just never know. Anyhow, the anchor held, and we were very happy sailors.

February 19, 1999

Today, we decided to take the trolley and locate West Marine. The head had been acting up, and I needed a part. The trolley dropped us off in downtown Ft. Myers Beach, which looked pretty interesting. We agreed to stop there for lunch after our West Marine purchase, which we did, and we found a cafe for a beer and a BLT while listening to a country western singer.

Walking back on the beach, we met a woman coming out of the water from her sunfish as the mast had broken. In five minutes, she told us her whole life story. She was seventy-four years of age, had five children, lived in Indiana next to Notre Dame, and had been coming down to Florida for eighteen years. At the age of fifty, she started sailing, skiing, and water skiing and loved them all. She was telling us all this, standing soaking wet in a shirt and bathing suit, never once complaining about being cold. When she heard we had sailed here and were on our way to Key West, she exclaimed that she would love to come with us, but she couldn't leave her husband as he wasn't well. Ann and I stood there spellbound, just listening. It was an amazing moment, and for some reason, we found ourselves exchanging phone numbers, maybe because she had such joie de vivre, and we wanted to know her better. It's hard to explain, but maybe one day she'll be at LaGuardia Airport giving us a call. Who knows?

We dinghied back to the boat and found a few more boats just arriving and about to set anchor. Within minutes of boarding *Perpetual*, a small sailboat started slipping toward us while a larger boat behind us was setting anchor. I immediately started the engine, thinking the larger boat had tripped our anchor, and as I put *Perpetual* in reverse, I heard a loud knocking sound. Oh no! Had the line gotten tangled on the prop, or was the transmission slipping? All I knew was I did not know the answer, so I quickly turned the engine off and hoped the anchor would reset as the smaller sailboat took off. Meanwhile, the larger sailboat was still working on anchoring when a woman yelled from the cockpit, "I'm sorry if we tripped your anchor." Maybe they did, maybe they didn't, maybe that knocking noise was a porpoise saying hello. All we wanted to do was stop, and so we did, hoping for the best. We were given a reprieve, time enough to have a wee spot of wine and some well-deserved dinner. Then suddenly, we were face to face or, more precisely, stern to bow with our new neighbors. Our anchor line had again wrapped around the keel, and as it released, it allowed *Perpetual* to totally let go and meet *Extra Sea* at a very inopportune moment. It was dark and quite windy. We handed our new neighbor our boat hook to fend off so we could pull up and reset our anchor, which we did in a matter of minutes, and thank God it was holding.

It was time to crawl into our v-berth for a not-so-restful sleep, but at least we were in a prone position.

February 20, 1999

Woke up groggy but grateful that our anchor held. *Extras Sea's* Captain dinghied over with our boat hook and again apologized for tripping our anchor. We thanked him for all his help in fending us off and got ready to abandon ship for the day and head for the beach.

All looked well on our return, and we had an uneventful Saturday night.

February 21, 1999

The sound of *Extra Sea's* engine woke us as they headed out, and we were glad it did. Originally, we were planning to stay another day, but after listening to the weather, today would be a better day for our trek to Naples. So, without further delay, we were off.

Out on the Gulf, it was glorious! The turquoise calm seas made it so.

Coming into Gordon's Pass could be difficult, as our trusty Waterway Guide indicated. It's where the Gulf of Mexico meets Naples Bay through rock jetties, and we were very careful to hug the starboard side of the channel, as instructed. Thankfully, five miles later, we were at the spot where the Town of Naples offers free moorings; however, all were taken. Out came our trusty Bruce anchor, and since we are tucked into a little cove with hopefully little current, we felt ok.

February 25, 1999

I can't believe it's been two months since Christmas. How fast time is flying, and we're still loving this life. It's a cool evening, and I just had a glorious warm shower. Ann is writing emails, and it's just so pleasant sitting down below in my warm sweats as the sun sets, creating a beautiful pink sky.

We have had a wonderful four-day stay in Naples. Our anchor held, and even when a free mooring was available, we decided to stay put. We dinghied our bikes into the town dock and toured all over.

The city is very upscale and has a beautiful downtown with areas both old and new. Some of the surrounding homes are quite modest and unpretentious, but out on the Gulf Drive, it's another story- grand homes with spectacular views. We found a tennis club where we paid the non-member fee of $15 and enjoyed an hour and a half of great rallies. Ann is getting quite good, I might add. We found Winns Market, which has been around for over fifty years, and stocked up on some needed items. Spent a relaxing day on the beach, rode three miles out of town to the post office, met some interesting folks hanging out on the dock doing wash, and worked out our strategy for our upcoming trip to Key West. We even managed to find a diver who cleaned *Perpetual*'s bottom.

One of the highlights of our Naples stay was sitting topside and watching what we later found out was the filming of a movie scene. A woman on a yacht was receiving a large box of flowers tied with a red bow. We then saw the man deliver another box of flowers, followed by the woman returning the flowers. Ann and I speculated that perhaps it was a wedding about to occur and the flowers were the wrong color, maybe the wrong flowers, or maybe they weren't flowers after all but a cover for a clandestine endeavor. We were having a field day with our conclusions. However, after the same scene occurred over and over again, we couldn't take it any longer. We finally hopped in the dinghy and found the film crew doing their thing as we sat and had a great laugh at ourselves.

February 26, 1999

It's quite a mystical moment sitting topside anchored off this tiny Coconut Island, watching the sun descend into the Gulf and hearing the surf hitting the sand. It reminds me of being with our friends Joan and Evie, who made it a ritual to gather with everyone and watch the sunsets every night when we visited them in Bradenton Beach. Out in the distance, I can see two sailboats coasting along in a calm sea. Hard to believe that New York got hit with a foot of snow, and here we are luxuriating in a southern sunset. It's Friday night, and if we were home, the fire would be blazing, and yes, that too renders a feeling of well-being, but this is incredible, and to boot, a dolphin just appeared. Thank you, God, for this splendor!

February 27, 1999

We dinghied into Coconut Island, which was only about fifty yards away. What a sweet little island just big enough for a short stroll as we drank our morning coffee while collecting shells.

After our morning pause, we decided to pull anchor and venture into Marco Island. We found a new anchorage in Factory Bay, where we recognized some other boats that had been in Naples. We heard that *Message in a Bottle* was playing in the local theater, so since we both had finished reading the book, it was a must-see for a Sunday matinee tomorrow.

Bikes were lowered into the dinghy, and off we went to do some exploring and much-needed provisioning. We found the location of the movie theater, about three and a half miles out of town, and then onto the Winn Dixie supermarket, where we stocked up on food for our journey down to the keys. Marco Island does not have the appeal of Naples, but it has a nearby movie theater.

Back on *Perpetual*, it was an Italian feast of spaghetti and meatballs, a little Merlot, and candlelight.

February 28, 1999

Today was our first Sunday Matinee, and as an extra bonus, it was a dinner theater. What a treat, as we were famished. The movie was enjoyable but not as good as the book, which is usually the case.

Back on board, it was an early bedtime after a bowl of soup and a quick read of the Times.

The front is arriving tonight, and hopefully, we are a "go" for the a.m.

March 1, 1999

What a windy night we experienced. Woke up to a large sailboat passing our bow in the wee hours of the morning. I feared that our anchor had been tripped and wound up staying awake to check our position until I could no longer keep my eyes open. Shortly after, I heard Ann listening to the weather. There were small craft advisories, but no hazardous conditions were reported, with northeast winds of 15-20. We should be able to handle this, we both agreed.

After fueling up and getting ice, we were off through Capri Pass Inlet out into the Gulf. We could see whitecaps breaking on the shoals.

We were feeling good to have at least done the Gulf a few times on calm days because today was going to be a challenge. Our GPS would be our reliable companion as we pressed "go to" from Red Buoy 2. The seas were mighty steep from behind, and we were traveling fast. After our coffee break was abruptly interrupted with coffee all over the deck, we regrouped, pulled out the genoa, and surfed in a more graceful fashion. Shortly after, Ann broke the bridge of her glasses. My navigator would definitely have a hard time reading the charts now. Fortunately, our GPS found each buoy and guided us into the most un Florida-type anchorage, one of the 10,000 islands that are totally uninhabited and surrounded by mangroves. We had left buoy #2 at 10 a.m. and arrived at 4:35. There were about five other boats anchored that had plenty of swing room, so that felt comfortable.

Ann just fixed her glasses with blue tape as I announced, "You are now quite a spectacle." We needed to laugh after our challenging day, and that we did.

March 2, 1999

Up bright and early after literally feeling comatose all night. It's amazing how the wind and sea are such potent hypnotics.

After our morning coffee, we pulled up the anchor and were off. It was only 8 a.m. Our destination was the Little Shark River. Our next marker was supposed to be red; however, we picked a green one and hit the ground. Luckily, the current was strong, and with a hard throttle in reverse, we were off and found the red and the green. It was my turn for a healthy dose of humility.

Out in the gulf, it was like a calm lake. It's amazing how quickly it can change. Just yesterday, we had water coming across our beam, and today just ripples against the hull. It was a very solitary sail with maybe a couple of boats way out on the horizon. We took turns showering in the cockpit and thoroughly enjoyed a beautiful day. As we approached our anchorage, which our guide described as being protected by sixty-foot mangroves, the thoughts of snakes and alligators began to creep into my mind. Ann remarked that I was deciding to worry about the "ridiculous." Having no other option, I was willing to be convinced that snakes don't swim and alligators can't climb, even if I didn't really buy it.

It's a beautiful, cool evening, and the smell of hot dogs and Ann's potato salad permeating from the cabin is a wonderful distraction.

THE HORRIFIC STORM ENCOUNTER

March 3, 1999

We awoke early to listen to the weather, which reported a chance of thunderstorms later in the day. Ann thought we could make it to Everglades Park before the storm, but I thought we should stay another day. We had no sightings of snakes or alligators last evening, and thunderstorms could be a major concern. My navigator was not convinced, especially when she pointed out that other boats were leaving. So we made the decision to leave but would leave later in the morning as we needed some higher water in the channel to avoid going aground. We had approximately twenty-five miles to Flamingo, and the marina had instructed us to come in on a rising tide which would be in the afternoon.

The day was quite gray, and the seas very calm. It had an eerie beauty to it, and I had just finished saying, " This seems ok."

I was down below when Ann exclaimed, "I just saw lightning! Take the helm." We were about one and a half miles offshore, and our GPS had us following a course to a marker off Middle Cape. Ann went down below to listen to the weather, which was now updated to hazardous conditions, gusts over 40, and water spouts.

We donned our life jackets, and the winds started churning up like nothing I had ever seen before. Within minutes, we were in a full-blown gale. The steel bar from the bimini became loose and was flailing dangerously in the cockpit as the dinghy was catapulting out of the water and crashing into the side of the boat. I had to get to the wheel as the keel was hitting bottom with a loud crash, and we had to get into deeper water. I tethered myself to avoid going overboard and crawled on the cockpit floor so I could attempt to reattach the bar. The waves were incredible. Meanwhile, Ann was down below, radioing the Coast Guard for help. I think we both thought we could die. Key West Coast Guard is pretty far away, and they announced they could not come as the storm was too bad, "Is there anyone we can call for you?" We would have to get through this on our own, and of course, we could use some help from the heavens as I kept saying "please," trying for the third time to reattach the bar. I noticed the zipper had opened, so if I could just safely remove the bar completely, that would solve that problem, which, thankfully, it did. I was now able to stand up and grab the wheel. The waves were crashing over the stern, and we needed to retrieve the hatch covers so the cabin wouldn't get swamped. The depth sounder said we were only in ten feet of water, and we were debating whether to throw down an anchor, but with the sea being so rough, it didn't feel like it was a good option. Every so often, I got an opportunity to put the throttle in forward and get us out further into deeper water. Just then, it seemed to let up a bit, so we decided to make a run for it, and that's literally what we did.

We were running with the wind behind us and surfing with the waves. There was no more lightning, and although it was windy, the worst was over. It was four hours later that we pulled into Flamingo Marina. We were absolutely exhausted but, oh, so thankful to be alive. We lost an oar, a flag pole, and a Christmas tree plant. Ann's secure knot-tying kept everything else in place, especially the dinghy.

Later that evening, we gathered on the dock with fellow sailors who had been in the storm. One man reported gusts of 60, and I knew I saw 39 on my wind instrument as I struggled on the cockpit floor. Somehow, it felt so good just talking about it all and being on land, knowing it was over and we were alive.

March 4 and 5, 1999

Flamingo was a wonderful place to take a break, and we definitely needed a break!!

Since it is part of the Everglades National Park, it has not only a marina but also cottages and motel-type rooms. There were many tourists, especially German-speaking people who, we were told, were given discounted fares to visit the Everglades.

The Visitor's Center was staffed by park rangers, and it made me think of my son, Patrick, who attended a forest ranger school in Wanakena, NY, and all the fascinating things he must have learned.

We biked the trails and walked around Echo Pond, which is a bird sanctuary that is amazingly peaceful and has lots of serious birders. We, on the other hand, could only identify the snowy egrets and the striking blue herons, but the walk was so calming and just what the nurse ordered after the previous day.

That night, we treated ourselves to a magnificent feast, and I sampled Pompano for the first time, which was delicious. Ann had shrimp, and we both delighted in a wonderful evening, again recounting our experience and focusing on gratitude for being alive. Ann thanked me for being her brave captain.

The next morning, Ann signed up for a canoe trip through the Everglades. There was only room for one, and that was fine with me. Being face-to-face with alligators is not very appealing. However, when it was time to go, the park ranger said she could fit another person, and since she would be in the canoe with us, I figured, what the heck, I might as well get over my alligator fear.

There were six canoes, and having Nancy, the tour guide in ours, was very reassuring. Ann was in front, and I was supposed to be the steering person. I must say that Nancy was not only knowledgeable but had a great sense of humor and the patience of a saint since my steering left a lot to be desired.

It was incredibly fascinating as we sighted bald eagles, birds called kites, storks, and oh so many alligators, some just basking on the shoreline and others slowly making their way through the shallow water but not into our canoe.

It was a very exciting trip, and as far as my alligator fear is concerned, I'm not sure if that was conquered; however, I came face to face with many, and I'm still here.

After having pizza at a cafe and listening to a mellow guitar player, it was time to prepare for our journey back on the water. I can't say it was not without some apprehension.

March 6, 1999

Woke very early at 5:30, the earliest since we left Kings Point, NY, to go through Hellgate on the second day of our trip. Today, we have to have a high tide to get out, and even with that, it would only be six feet. We watched the beautiful golden sunrise and said a morning prayer. Shortly after, we were aground, but thankfully, with some surges to the throttle, we were off and out in the bay.

It was then we noticed the exhaust wasn't putting out the same volume of water that it previously had, and when we saw white smoke, I became very concerned and went down below to check the engine, which seemed hotter than usual even though the alarm wasn't sounding we decided to lower the throttle, and that's when the alarm started blaring so off went the engine as Ann hoisted the main and pulled out the genoa. We had 7 knots of wind behind us, so we hoped to sail most of the way and only use the engine when we arrived at Marathon.

There were a plethora of lobster buoys, and we tried carefully to avoid them. I was down below when I heard a loud thump. Ann was at the helm and thought we might have hit something. It was a few minutes later that Ann reported she couldn't steer the boat and asked me to take over. She was absolutely right, as we were not moving. I thought perhaps the cable that attached the wheel to the rudder had snapped. So we decided to remove the wheel and affix the emergency tiller, all the while chastising ourselves for not having practiced this before we actually needed it. For a brief moment, we thought we had steerage but no such luck, so we must have gotten caught up on one of the lobster buoys. The time was now 1 p.m., and we were hours from Marathon with no other boats in sight. Time to call Tow Boat

US. Neither one of us is brave enough to risk diving into what could be shark territory.

The good news is that our trusty GPS pinpointed our exact coordinates, and Tow Boat US found us easily. After diving and releasing some of the tangled buoys, our diver announced he couldn't release all, so it was time to secure the tow lines and head off to Marathon,

A few hours later, we were safely tucked into a dock at Key Boatworks, where we were told it wouldn't be till Monday that someone could look at our boat. That was fine with us. Having been up since dawn, it was time to just stop, and that's what we did.

March 8 and 9, 1999

Living in a boatyard is quite different from living in a marina, especially now that *Perpetual* was out of the water. Using the ladder to get on and off the boat in the wee hours of the night to visit the head was a bit of a challenge. Happy to report no incidents occurred.

On Monday, we met Roger, who had already looked at our steering and found nothing wrong except a missing pin, which, incidentally, I had. The cable had not broken, and the offending lobster buoy that had been tangled on the prop was easily removed with no evidence of prop damage. We were more than pleased. Roger was delightful, as well as a competent mechanic. He told us he was sixty-five and had three heart attacks followed by bypass surgery. He then went on to report he loved his cigars and always looked forward to the end of the work day when he would enjoy a good smoke with his beer. He was telling us this as he was curled up like a pretzel on the cockpit floor, checking the engine. In the meantime, Ann and I were standing by in case he needed CPR. He didn't, thank God, and the beat-up impeller he found was replaced. That was fortunate as the impeller sucks up the sea water and cools the engine. He would come back in the morning to change the oil. We thanked Roger and felt so relieved that *Perpetual* would be afloat again soon.

Back on our bikes, we found Inflatable Boats where we could order an oar from Quicksilver, the dealer who made our dinghy, and pick it up on the return from Key West easily enough.

Now it was off to Publix, where everyone seemed to be a boater, easily identified in shorts, T-shirts, docksiders, and the telltale baseball cap, all carrying mounds of groceries in canvas satchels. Leaving the store, we ran into a couple we had first met in Elizabeth City, North Carolina, and then later in Vero Beach. They had just returned from the Keys and told us how crowded the anchorages were and that most of them lacked protection. They had found one spot that offered some protection and drew us a diagram of its location. Boaters are so helpful. We thanked them and bid farewell.

Off to Key West tomorrow?

March 10, 1999

We decided not to go the full distance to Key West today since we needed to make sure all was well with the engine, and we wanted to find the Moser Channel.

Out in the Florida Bay, it was very shallow and not very well marked. Our destination was Bahia Honda, a state park that had a nice beach. Up ahead, we spotted a sailboat with a hailing port of Plymouth, England. They, too, were feeling some confusion as the buoys were not coinciding with the chart. My trusty navigator yelled over to them that our Waterway Guide had revealed that new markers had been placed, and we would try and find the way if they wished to follow.

"That would be lovely," said the Captain in his melodious English accent.

In spite of my doubts, we led the way splendidly up the channel under a bridge that presented its own challenge as it ran parallel with the old bridge and created an optical illusion. Nonetheless, all went well, as we heard over our radio, "Thanks, *Perpetual,* well done." They were now off to Marathon as we hollered "Cheerio." Again, my navigator saved the day.

We were now in the Hawk Channel, where our navigation had to be very precise since a Coral Reef offers the only protection from the Atlantic Ocean. We had already set our GPS with the waypoints, and all we had to do was push "go to," and we were in business.

It was a couple of hours later that we were heading toward the old Bahia Honda Bridge, which, by the way, is a historic national monument and has a section cut out to allow sailboats to enter. We anchored right off the beach between the two bridges and decided to set two anchors because of the stiff current. This was a first for us, and it meant checking and rechecking our fix throughout the evening and night. The stars were magnificent, though, as we took turns peering out the v-berth hatch on our nightly watches.

ARRIVAL IN KEY WEST

March 12, 1999

We wanted to spend the day at the beach, but after listening to the weather, it sounded like it would be in our best interests to head off to Key West before the weekend, as the weather could be stormy.

Arrival in Key West

We pulled up our two trusty anchors, which incidentally did an incredible job, and we were on our way. It was very hot with not much wind, but fortunately, the diesel sounded great, and even though we barely sailed, our short trip was pleasant enough.

Entering Key West Harbor was such an exciting thrill. A Celebrity cruise ship to starboard and a plethora of boats anchored throughout the harbor. We quickly located the diagram of the anchorage our fellow boater friend had drawn and proceeded cautiously. Even though it seemed far from town, we found a small space and set our two an-chors. By now, we had names for the two, Big Bruce and Dainty Danny.

We will see the town tomorrow. For now, it is an amazing feeling to revel in the realization that we are here in the most southern part of the USA.

The sunset is spectacular, and one of our fellow anchor neighbors is basking in the nude. This must be KEY WEST!!

March 13, 1999

Off to town in the dinghy. It's a long, wet ride, but worth it. It was late morning, and the bar scene was already happening. Sloppy Joe's was packed as a band played lively music. A little too early for us to partake, so we opted for a small outdoor cafe called Billy's and had a nice lunch followed by a trolley tour through town. It was fun being tourists in such a lively town. The Hemingway House would be a must-see, but not today. We have decided to basque in the frivolity of Key West for a few days, and there would be plenty of time to visit Mr. Hemingway's abode.

Our dinghy ride back was long, bumpy, and wet. So happy to be back in our warm cabin. Listening to the weather confirmed the arrival of an approaching cold front and also the possibility of thundershowers in the morning. We battened everything we could and hoped our anchors would be on top of their game.

March 14 and 15, 1999

The next two days seem somewhat of a blur. Since there was rela-tively no protection with the gulf on one side and the Atlantic Ocean on the other, waves were breaking over the bow as we huddled in our cozy cabin, hoping and praying for a reprieve. The good news was that we were not alone, and our fellow neighbors were both caring and helpful. One sailboat, smaller than ours, was now in the mangrove. His anchor hadn't held, but by morning, people dinghied in to offer assistance. They were trying to get him off in the high tide but to no avail. It wasn't until Tuesday morning that he was safely anchored again. There was another Pearson 28 on a mooring whose owner, a South African, offered his advice as we were contemplating the integrity of our anchors. He thought we were sitting "pretty." Our nude neighbor, a few boat lengths away, had now donned clothes and dinghied over to see if we needed anything. They both radioed us that night again to offer assistance if needed. It was so comforting to know that there were very helpful people around as we swallowed Bonnine to ward off the nausea that accompanied the bouncing motion of the seas.

Anchored in Key West

I knew I probably hit a low water mark when, in the middle of the night, Ann and I were checking anchors, and I inadvertently locked her in the head. The door had been swinging, so I naturally hinged it shut, not seeing her balancing on the bowl. Oh well, our framed portrait on the door, which reads, "Blessed are we who can laugh at ourselves for we shall never cease to be amused," took on a real meaning. And in the midst of queasy stomachs and tinges of fear, we were able to laugh and thank God for that.

Listening to the VHF was quite another scene. A mayday was called by a guy who had been shot in the head with a pellet gun. The Coast Guard responded to put pressure on the wound and then asked if he could come ashore to meet the paramedics. He confirmed he was with someone who could dinghy him to shore. Then, a while later, a call from the same party again asked where the paramedics were. Apparently, they went to the wrong dock. Since we heard no more communication, we assumed that he finally got the help he needed.

Then, there was a heart-wrenching communication between a child who was on a boat calling his mom at work and saying that someone threw up. Mom was not very reassuring, and she told the poor kid not to worry about it, that his brother would soon be there, and not to call her at work. It was a dark stormy night, and two grown-ups on *Perpetual* were scared. We couldn't imagine how that poor little kid felt.

March 16, 1999

When we woke Tuesday morning after a rather restless night, we were fairly close to our new neighbor who was yelling, *"Perpetual."* We quickly reacted and were on deck in minutes, trying to reset our anchors. We had let out more lines the previous night, and it wasn't that it dragged but that it changed our position. After a good hour, we were reset with ample distance between boats.

Our anchors had taken on personalities during the first few hours of storm duty two days ago. I took to drawing faces on my hands, naming them Bruce and Danny, and proceeded to do a puppet show complete with anchor dialogue. It kept me amused as Ann chuckled periodically. Maybe it was the Bloody Mary; nevertheless, it passed the time and put us in better coping moods.

The sky was now blue, the water calm, and we were determined to go ashore.

We enjoyed touring the Hemingway House and had a delicious lunch at the Rooftop. It was beyond wonderful to be walking on land and not bouncing in a turbulent sea. The contrast makes one feel so appreciative.

Happy St Patrick's Day, March 17, 1999

How fun and exciting to be in a tropical climate for the wearing of the green. The town was already bustling with Irish energy, and it seemed fitting to partake in the joyous festivities, so of course, we had to have one beer at Sloppy Joe's while an Irish group sang away. It would only be one as we had not eaten breakfast, so off we went to Bagatelles, where we had a gourmet delight, sitting on the deck watching all the goings on.

The day was grand, and we'll always remember our St. Paddy's Day in Key West.

March 18, 1999

We are again back in town provisioning and purchasing Key West caps and new docksiders, as my current ones have lost their grip. We found a quiet end of town and wrote postcards while munching on some NY pizza.

Back on *Perpetual,* it was time to enjoy our last Key West sunset. Wow, we never tire of this life; even though it was only a few days ago, we felt different.

March 19, 1999

Picked up our two brave anchors, Danny and Bruce, and after stopping by the fuel dock, we were off, leaving memorable Key West Harbor behind.

Out on the Hawk channel, the wind was blowing, which allowed a nice sail for a while, but then we were beating too close and had to turn the engine on. Our destination was Bahia Honda since we hadn't had the opportunity to explore the beach on our trip south.

Approaching Bahia Honda became confusing as we were heading for the wrong bridge. I had to throttle down to get my bearings, and when I tried to throttle up, the engine seemed to be very sluggish. It also looked like the old black smoke was coming out of the exhaust again, which was not good. I silently prayed, and we finally found the correct bridge with the opening. I was hoping our low-throttle engine would be able to negotiate the stiff current. It miraculously did, and we entered the anchorage only to find eight other boats. We set our two trusty anchors and hoped for the best. We will think about the engine problems tomorrow. For now, it is an anchor watch since the wind is kicking, and we are fairly close to the bridge.

March 20, 1999

We were both very tired, not sleeping much, as we took turns checking the anchors. As soon as we saw another boat break anchor, we, too, decided to pull up ours and reset so we wouldn't be so close to the bridge. However, we were now too close to another boat and decided to reset again, only to get tangled in another boat's anchor line.

The poor Canadian Captain was rudely awakened when *Perpetual* made a close call to his vessel. It was time to detangle as Ann laid out all the lines, and the Canadian gent, with his boat hook, did the magic. Now, for hopefully the last time, we set our anchors. We hadn't had our morning coffee yet, and it felt like it should be Miller Time. So we took a moment of reprieve, sipping coffee and watching our anchors until we felt confident that Danny and Bruce were doing well.

We dinghied into a very small but perfectly accommodating Marina, which is part of the state park and right off a delightful beach. A weekend crowd was present, but we found a nice spot, and we spent the afternoon taking naps and wading in the turquoise-blue water. *Perpetual* was only about a hundred yards from us, and Danny and Bruce were performing perfectly. They knew we were watching.

That night, with the winds calmer, we had a very restful sleep and awoke to another beautiful Florida day. We packed a lunch and dinghied onto the beach, where we settled into a thrilling game of Scrabble. Incidentally, I won for a change. Yes!!

Back on *Perpetual*, it was time to tackle our engine troubles, so we cleaned out the saltwater strainer which was chock-full of grass. That was probably the culprit, we hoped, and feeling a bit more relieved, we planned to head back to Marathon in the a.m.

Monday, March 22, 1999

Up bright and early as we wanted to do a more thorough check of the engine before lifting the anchor. The water coming out of the Exhaust was minimal, and there were streaks of black smoke. We then called Keys Boatworks and spoke to Roger, who told us to try and open the sea cocks that fed the strainer to see if water was coming in. There was not a drop, so therefore, the thru-hull was probably clogged with seagrass. That settled it, so we radioed Tow Boat US and were happy to hear Captain Steve's voice. He would be here in thirty minutes. In the meantime, we successfully pulled up one anchor, so by the time he came, we knew the routine as we bridled the front cleats with his towboat lines and then retrieved our second anchor.

We made our way safely back to Keys Boat Yard with the help of Tow Boat US and were met by Roger, who greeted us like long-lost relatives. He would check everything out in the morning, and for now, we should just relax, so we did.

For the next three days, we again frequented Publix to replenish food and ice. We biked up and down Route 1 and found a West Marine, where we picked up our new dinghy oar that we had lost in the horrific storm. The great thing about Marathon is that everything is readily accessible, and we certainly needed the exercise.

Back at the boatyard, Roger checked out the engine for any further damage as, indeed, the thru-hull was clogged with grass, which necessitated the boat being pulled so he could clear it completely and install a strainer to prevent a recurrence. Our insurance had covered the previous work; however, this new situation would be on us. We had total confidence in Roger's assessment and plan. So, for tonight, *Perpetual* and her crew will be landlubbers.

THREADING OUR WAY BACK TO THE EAST COAST VIA THE KEYS

March 25, 1999

Perpetual was now back in the water, and it was time to pack up our bikes and bid farewell to Roger. The engine sounded great, with clear water spouting from the exhaust. We found a nice place to anchor on the other side of Marathon with plenty of room to swing. There were three other sailboats with at least ten teenage boys aboard each. They were having a blast doing cannonballs into the pristine clear water. Tranquil, it was not, but safe, it was.

March 26, 1999

The weather was looking somewhat threatening, with some scary clouds over Marathon. Upon listening to NOAA, there was a report of water spouts with an explanation of what to do if you spotted one. "Move in a ninety-degree angle." Since we were still at anchor, we decided to wait a while and get an update later. Having experienced that terrifying thunderstorm earlier this month, we are extremely conscientious of any mention of threats.

At ten, we got an update on possible thunderstorms in the Miami metropolitan area. We decided that was far enough away to safely leave And ventured out again on the Hawk channel.

Our destination was Indian Key. It was late afternoon that we finally set Bruce in a fairly unprotected Anchorage with absolutely no other boats or, for that matter, no other trace of civilization around. It was a bit eerie, to say the least, as we tried not to think about it and tentatively ate our leftover ziti and crawled into our bunk, hoping sleep would overcome us and the morning would arrive soon.

March 27, 1999

We awoke to a beautiful Saturday morning complete with the wind that would favor our point of sail. I was naturally concerned about fuel consumption, not that we had an immediate need, but according to the waterway guide, there were very few places we could fill up.

We headed for Key Largo and enjoyed a most beautiful sail. There was a marina that we could get into. The approach was dicey as it was at the end of a canal. When we finally found it, we topped off the diesel and got some much-needed water and ice. It's amazing how these little things give one such peace of mind.

Outside off the Hawk Channel, we found Rodriquez Key, where we anchored with at least five other boats. It was nice to have company with plenty of room to swing. It was a one-anchor night, and Bruce was on duty.

March 28, 1999

Another fantastic sailing day winds at 12 to 15 kn, and we were booking. Our destination was Caesar Creek. Basically, we had no choice as the whole area was totally remote. It was a long way off the channel, and the approach was sketchy as there were no markers and our trusty Waterway Guide wanted us to "avoid the shoal by reading the water," which we tried and failed but managed to find the shoal with the stern of the boat being in at least five feet of water, and the bow in only two feet. A kind fisherman tried to pull us off, but to no avail. We were quite tired from a pretty hard day of sailing, and I could feel my patience waning. Our first instinct was to throw the anchor out kedge our way off, but then we decided to hoist the main, and that was just what we needed as we sailed off the shoal into Caesar Creek (Shit's Creek), as we renamed it. It would be a two-anchor night at this very remote creek with no other boats and surrounded by mangroves. We were both too tired to worry, had something to eat, and fell asleep.

March 29, 1999

Our two anchors did the job and avoided the mangroves. Our coping mechanisms were back intact after replenishing much-needed sleep and a great cup of coffee. We carefully avoided the nasty shoal and backed out on the Hawk channel. We hoisted sail, turned off the engine, and ripped through the ocean swells. It was a magnificent sail, probably our best yet, as *Perpetual* clocked 7.6 mph more than once. It was work holding the wheel but thoroughly exhilarating, and in the distance was Key Biscayne with the backdrop of Miami Harbor. Somehow, it felt comforting to be heading to a less remote destination. We found the state park, anchored *Perpetual*, and toasted ourselves to being in Miami.

Tomorrow, we head into a marina close to South Beach. We hadn't been in a marina in a very long time, and the thought alone was a treat.

Match 30, 1999

A short trip but so exhilarating as we headed into Government Cut, where all the cruise ships dock and also those moving apartment buildings we hadn't seen in a very long time but seriously didn't miss. The wind was blowing 15-20 right in our face, making the water very choppy. Alas, we found the Miami Beach Marina and were thrilled to pull into our floating slip. It was only lunchtime, so we opted for a Bloody Mary with our cheese sandwich. We are so thrilled to be in an upscale marina.

It was now time to unload our bikes and explore South Beach. Ann had been here in December with Marie and Carol after taking Jordan back to the airport, and she was so excited showing me all the places they had been. The place is so lively and fun. The Art Deco flavor is so colorful and delightfully gay, and we felt right at home. Saw Versace's villa and had an early supper at the News Café, which was bustling, providing a stage of characters for people watching. We just love this place.

March 31, 1999

Donna and her new friend Pat are meeting us for dinner tonight, so we spent most of the day cleaning *Perpetual* and ourselves, enjoying warm showers after a swim in the pool.

Donna and Pat arrived. It was a wonderful reunion, and it was especially nice to meet Pat. We walked down to South Beach to a great Italian restaurant and just talked and laughed and laughed as we reminisced about old times and caught up with their new times. We couldn't believe that it was midnight, a first for us since New Year's.

April 5, 1999

Yes, we're still hanging out in South Beach and currently sitting at our favorite, The News Café, for the umpteenth time, awaiting lunch.

Since my last entry, we left the marina and found a wonderful anchorage only a mile away. The price was right, and besides, too much Marina comfort can spoil us. We are now anchored with a group of French Canadians, and the French-speaking, especially from the children, is quite delightful to hear, and we are only a bike ride away from everything.

Ann's grandparents used to live off Collins Avenue, and it was fun exploring and actually finding where they lived when they retired. On the way, we passed the Eden Roc and the Fontainebleau, sneaking in for a bathroom break in the posh Fontainebleau.

Since it was Passover, bicycling was not easy since everyone was walking. On Saturday, we had a beach day with thousands of others. We have been truly spoiled, having found beaches with so few people up to now. Easter Sunday was spent enjoying brunch at our favorite café and feasting on Easter eggs Benedict. Then off to a movie in downtown Miami, where we enjoyed *Analyze This*.

We just now made reservations to fly out to San Francisco from Charlotte, NC, for Erin's graduation from Chiropractic School. The plan is to be in New Bern at Uncle Frank's by June 7 so we can be in Charlotte by June 12.

April 6, 1999

We finally picked up the anchor and bid a fond farewell to South Beach. Off to Fort Lauderdale for a rendezvous with Iris. She and Donna now have separate homes. Sounds like everything is OK between them, so that's the main thing, as we will be staying with them both on separate occasions.

It was a fairly busy approach passing the large ship Channel at Port Everglades, and just the normal boat traffic waiting for the various bridges to open was a bit draining.

It was a great relief to find the Fort Lauderdale municipal marina, where moorings are $15 per day and one left for *Perpetual*. So fortuitous since we will be frolicking on land while staying with our friends in Delray Beach.

April 15, 1999

We are currently back on the water after a wonderful time.

Iris picked us up last Wednesday and welcomed us to her lovely new condo. She had a whole schedule of events planned, which would start with her hosting a gathering of friends in our honor. We were thoroughly touched, to say the least, and when she informed us that Donna and Pat were included, we were truly relieved. In spite of Iris and Donna's breakup, they were determined to remain friends.

The peace and tranquility of Iris's home, punctuated by lovely music and the view of the lake, was very enticing, and of course, having a real bed and chest of drawers just added to our delight. A highlight of our visit was the beautiful Sunday morning service at Unity Church, followed by brunch at The Sunday House.

Annie Feeney

Then, off to Donna and Pat's, where we laughed and laughed until the wee hours of the morning. We are not used to being up till 3 a.m. Nevertheless, we rallied and even learned to play black jack with Pat's patient tutelage.

The following day, we all decided to go out on the casino boat, which yielded no big wins but such an enjoyable evening.

Our clothes are in a pretty sorry state, and it's only when we are among non-boaters or back on land that we notice or even care. So when we hit Ross's department store, I even had fun picking out a dress for Erin's graduation. The problem is the extra twelve pounds that I have gained.

Pat, to the rescue! She is a lifelong member of Weight Watchers and was able to pick up all our point guides, but we would have to weigh in and attend a meeting, which we did. Thanks to Donna and Pat, we were able to provision ourselves with all the needed low-fat, non-fat essentials after first stopping at the Pier for our last normal lunch until we rendezvous again in Myrtle Beach at Pat's condo for Memorial Day weekend. So, for the next six weeks, we shall be counting points and hoping for the best.

Back to the present, the wind is really honking, but since it's behind, we are not experiencing it as hard as it would be if it was coming out of the north. We just passed the Two Georges Restaurant, where Donna, Ann, and I went several times last year when this trip was a mere dream. We even had lunch there this week with Pat and Donna and marveled at the empty space where the Ocean Avenue bridge had been and is no longer there. Now, here we are, waving to the people eating lunch as we sail by. Wow!!! This is a moment for deep thought and gratitude. Our dream has actually become our reality because just as the bridge is no longer there, so many things could have occurred that might have prevented the actualization of this moment. This trip has been such a gift, and there isn't a day that goes by when I don't quietly say thank you.

We planned to anchor in Lantana; however, the wind was now howling, and there were actual white caps at our stern. When we turned into the wind, it was blowing about 25 kn. There was no protection, and not one other boat was present. It was 4 p.m., the normal time for us to be stopping. The wiser decision was to move on, which we did, negotiating three more bascule bridges, giving us a total of twenty for the day. We arrived at Lake Worth just in time to watch the casino boat depart the harbor. Here, we found many boats, and after the second try in total darkness, our anchor took hold. It was now 8:30 when all was said and done, and time for our five-point dinner. On went the barbecue. We were exhausted but very hungry. As the latter won out, we devoured barbecue chicken, rice, and green beans and almost fell asleep on our plates. But we managed to move two more feet to our bunk for a comatose event.

April 17, 1999

We are sitting anchored in Peck Lake just off the ICW for the second time, having anchored here on the way to cross Lake Okeechobee. Yesterday's trek was the beginning of the repeat trip back home, and as we passed the Palm Beach Christmas house, the realization set in and provoked us to call the kids all except Jordan, whose number we don't have, and leave the message "we are on our way home." There was a certain sadness as we realized all good things come to an end. Although we will be on the water for another three months, we had indeed completed the journey into the unknown, and from this point on, we would be retracing our path homeward bound, but maybe with some side trips.

Peck Lake is a beautiful, serene anchorage, only a short dinghy ride to the shore, where across the dunes lies the ocean. We hadn't gone ashore on the last trip since the threat of thunderstorms in the vicinity had been announced by the Coast Guard, so we decided to stay put and explore the beach. The day was gray and cool as the north wind was blowing a steady 12 to 15 with gusts of 25. The ominous clouds kept us glued to the radio as we listened for marine updates on 16. There were numerous reports of vessels in trouble and thunderstorms in the surrounding areas—done that! Been there! We were perfectly happy sitting safely with at least three other boats in close proximity and our trusty Bruce keeping us out of the mangroves. It was actually pleasant having a sunless day, such an anomaly for Florida. We could hear thunder in the distance, and it did get gusty by the afternoon, but the scary clouds were gone, so ashore we went.

The storm in Peck Lake

It was almost mystical walking on the empty beach collecting shells, each of us in our own private reverie. Back on board *Perpetual*, it was time for a five-point dinner, and tonight, we could splurge on some wine. We were getting back to our sea routine and, by 8 p.m., tucked in the v-birth for our five minutes of reading before falling sound asleep.

April 18, 1999

Awoke to a cold cabin and hurriedly got the coffee going. The temperature has plummeted into the fifties. Ann picked up Bruce, which was caked with mud but kept us safe and secure. Out on the ICW, it was breezy but pleasant and quite beautiful. We approached the famous Cross Roads at the Saint Lucie inlet and reflected on how confused we were the first time, and now, having done it twice, what a difference it makes. In fact, when I think about all we've done and been through since then, it's amazing that we still not only enjoy the water but also each other.

We had a pleasant trip to Vero beach, where we picked up our assigned mooring and would probably be alone, not rafting up with a complete stranger. As we dinghied in, we reminisced, writing our Christmas cards here and finally getting into the Christmas spirit. Now, it was time to do some laundry and partake in hot showers.

April 19, 1999

We thought yesterday was cool, but today, the temperature is forty-five degrees, and it is probably much colder in the cabin. It was truly tortuous leaving the v-berth; however, we had to catch the trolley at the dock, which would take us to Publix for some needed items. Such a nice service, and it was very prompt with no charge. Quite a number of people provision here for the Bahamas, so it's probably a very profitable nicety in the long run.

Back on board, it was 11 a.m. as we prepared to get underway after stopping for fuel, water, and ice. A very pleasant trip, but sadly, the beautiful turquoise water has been left behind as we head into Central Florida. We anchored off a spoils island just as we had done on our voyage south. We called Perry and Joanne, our friends in Cocoa Beach, to tell them we'd love to see them if possible. We were thrilled to get a message from Perry insisting that we stay at their marina, where they purchased their new condo.

April 20, 1999

Out on the Indian river, we had an easy trip, pretty straightforward, but unfortunately, the wind was in our face, so on went the engine. Perry had given us a description of his new condo on the seventh floor of an eight-story building that was hard to miss as we turned to port. We radioed him as he said he would be monitoring his VHF, and there he was, standing on the pier waiting to take our lines just as he did when we first met him in Fernandina Beach. It was a wonderful reunion with him and Joanne. Their condo is spectacular, overlooking the Indian river. They couldn't have been more hospitable, giving us their key to the tennis courts and showers, which we took total advantage of. Perry made a call to John and Eileen back in NY, and we all took turns conversing.

That evening, we went out to dinner and enjoyed Mahi Mahi and scallops wrapped in bacon. No counting points tonight.

Joanne informed us that she had been recently diagnosed with hepatitis-C and was in a study using interferon and another drug. She also had a questionable Mammography and was planning to see the radiologist tomorrow. That seemed pretty intense to me, but Joanne has this wonderful calm attitude about life, and that has to have some positive effects; I only hope so.

We were going to stay one night at their dock; however, they insisted that we stay another and come to dinner tomorrow eve.

April 21, 1999

During our morning coffee, Joanne called and asked if we had heard about the Columbine shooting that happened yesterday. We had not, as she described the gruesome event. How awful for those families. Life is so precious, and why would anyone do something so horrific?

We took advantage of the tennis courts and later biked to the quaint CoCoa village.

That evening, Joanne reported that the radiologist was taking a wait-and-see approach, hearing this as good news.

Her sister and husband arrived, and we had a delightful evening of talking and laughing while enjoying the culinary delight Joanne and Perry had prepared. It was hard saying goodbye. They are both very special. We promised to keep in touch.

April 22, 1999

It was an early morning departure aboard *Perpetual,* as we had a long day ahead of us. Perry was on the dock, casting us off and out into the Indian River, our destination being Rockhouse Creek, some fifty miles away. Another beautiful blue sky day and just enough wind to pull out the Jib. It was late afternoon when we finally anchored and shared a "two-point" Bud Light as we prepared dinner.

The evening was purely mystical, watching and listening to dolphins as the sun set, casting a pink hue all over the western sky.

The next morning, we dinghied to the beach. Our friend Peggy, back in New York, had arranged a "prayer watch" for another friend who was having surgery, and we signed up for the 10-11 hour. What a beautiful spot to be quiet in prayer.

Later, we returned to *Perpetual* only to fix lunch and promptly returned to the beach, where we spent the rest of the day playing Scrabble. Another win for me-YES. Since this is not the usual, it needs to be celebrated.

April 24, 1999

Today, we were heading for our least favorite anchorage, the cement factory, but we had little choice. As we approached the area, a Coast Guard boat pulled out of nowhere and actually guided us into the deeper water, which was amazingly only about three feet from the shoreline. It truly felt like another little miracle, something we have experienced many times on this quite extraordinary journey.

We arrived at our anchorage, as we remembered it, next to a cement factory, and were thrilled to be the only boat, not very scenic but quite protected.

Time for Scrabble, where Ann scored seventy-nine points, a big win with "Priggish and Rin," a memorable win for her.

April 25, 1999

With a threat of afternoon thunderstorms, we were up early and out on the waterway, and it quickly turned cloudy and cool. According to our guide, it is one of the shallowest sections of the ICW. We were spared from either going aground or encountering any thunderstorms.

We arrived in picturesque St. Augustine and headed into a marina where we could take a luxurious shower, reprovision, and have a good walk around town.

April 26, 1999

We were able to hire a mechanic to change the oil and fuel filters. We spent most of the morning cleaning the boat and assisting the mechanic.

It was unbearably hot, so we opted for a bike ride to The Computer Cafe, which we discovered in December. We were surprised to find out it was no longer there. OK, off to the library, a few miles out of town. Usually, there is a cool breeze when riding our bikes, but we had no such luck today. The air-conditioned library was a welcome spot to just sit, read, and cool off.

That evening, we treated ourselves to an "almost" low-calorie dinner at an old tavern across from the marina. I had scrumptious Oysters Divine, and Ann opted for Grilled Grouper as we enjoyed a guitarist playing and singing Joni Mitchel songs.

April 27, 1999

We said farewell to Saint Augustine as we headed through the beautiful Lions Bridge. Ann pulled out the Jib, and we sailed all the way. How we love this!

We arrived at a new anchorage for us, the St George River, just off the ICW. The scene has definitely changed. We have left the big Florida condos and pricey homes and have returned to the serene marshlands.

We fired up our alcohol stove, fried some steak, onions, and peppers, and enjoyed our last night in Florida while sipping wine and reminiscing about our five-month stay.

May 3, 1999

Since my last entry, we have had spells of bad weather, cold, rainy, and windy. Our plan had been to bypass Fernandina Beach and head straight up the St Mary's River that would take us into Georgia. However, last Wednesday proved to be bleak with threats of thunderstorms, so it was a wise decision to anchor off Fernandina Beach and try to stay warm. The next day, although cloudy, no storm threats, so off we went, meandering up the St. Mary's River to Lang's marina, which became our home for four days.

The town of St Mary's is a quaint Rivertown with unpretentious restaurants serving delicious food. We sampled lunch at Lang's Seafood, and since the family is in the shrimping business, we enjoyed the freshest shrimp we probably will ever have in our lifetime. Whisper's Cafe was a treat for three days straight as we hid from the cold and dampness and regained some warmth with hot tea and sandwiches. The grocery store was about three and a half miles out of town, but we needed the exercise since our point counting had been ignored on several occasions. On the way back, we stopped at the local movie theater and saw *Life is Beautiful*, which moved us to tears. Just what we needed as we had been feeling a little bummed because of the weather, and that movie totally snapped us out of it.

We found a great little gift shop where we bought my daughter Lisa the most precious bear for her 30th birthday, which is less than a week away. Now that's hard to believe!! How fast the years fly by.

On our shop tour, we found a crafts store whose owner was quite hilarious and entertained us for at least an hour. By the time we left her shop, we knew her whole story and felt a sort of high from all the laughter.

I can't forget to mention our Friday late afternoon happy hour at Seagles, where an innocent martini and postcard writing became a four-hour marathon. It was such fun watching and conversing with the locals. However, those extra martinis, combined with chicken wings really did me in, and how happy I was to be finally tucked into our cold but welcome v-berth, vowing never to do that again. Ann had her own regrets as Tylenol came to the rescue on Saturday.

We are now anchored comfortably in Cumberland Island, and for the second time, it is just spectacular. It was only a ninety-minute sail here, and now it's time to barbecue some steaks. The sun has returned. We are here with three other sailboats, and life is so good.

May 5, 1999

Spent most of yesterday dealing with my tenant's nonpayment of rent. Actually, my daughter Lisa was the one dealing with it, and successfully, I might happily add. Having that off my plate, we dinghied into beautiful Cumberland Island and spent our last day on the pristine beach playing Scrabble. Not a winning day for me, but a good game nonetheless.

Today, we are on our way to Jekyll Island, but the forecast of a forty percent chance of thunderstorms gave us pause for concern since we would be crossing the Cumberland River and St Andrew's Sound—

almost in the mighty Atlantic Ocean. There was, however, an alternative route, which our Waterway Guide described as a better run in bad weather. The downside, though, was that there were a few areas that were very shallow and that with an eight-foot tide, we should be taking it on in rising tide. We decided to take our chances with the depth, better than experiencing thunderstorms on the high seas.

After a good forty-five minutes of pulling up Danny and Bruce, we were off bidding a final farewell to Cumberland Island. By the time we arrived at the turn-off, which would take us through a maze of creeks and a land cut for almost fifteen miles, the sky was very gray, and the rain was beginning. It was truly beautiful but a solitary passage winding through the desolate marshes with absolutely no other boats or, for that matter, any sign of human life visible. There were, however, alligators. At first, I thought I saw a piece of bark approaching our bow. As we got closer, we saw the eyes of not one but two alligators. Of course, I won't deny our quiet terror as we were now approaching Umbrella Cut, the worst of the shoal areas, and if we went aground, could these creatures crawl aboard *Perpetual*? Many prayers were said, and thanks to our guardian angels, we found more than enough water to avoid these visitors.

Jekyll Harbor Marina was only three miles away!

May 6, 1999

Jekyll Island is another magnificent island we never would have known about had we not ventured out to sea. We biked all over.

In the historic district sits the Jekyll Island Club Hotel, which was the retreat for millionaires such as Goodyear, Morgan, Vanderbilt, and Rockefeller. They formed an exclusive club that was inaccessible to the rest of the world until the State of Georgia purchased it and, later on, in the 70s, opened it to the public. The indoor tennis court is still intact. Croquet is played on the front lawn, and mandatory white is the uniform of the day. It was such a thrill just meandering about and playing tourist.

Later on, we biked over to the ocean and found a restaurant that rescued our famished appetites. The sky began to look stormy as we left the restaurant. Within minutes, it was hailing as we pedaled quickly and made it back to the Jekyll Island Hotel, where we sat safely on the porch rockers with the paying guests, watching the lightning and teeming rain. It was only a short reprieve, however, as we remembered that we had left the ports open on *Perpetual*.

After mopping up ourselves and *Perpetual*, it was time for some hot vegetable soup and a good night's sleep.

May 7, 1999

The weather forecast sounded iffy for the next few days, with chances of thunderstorms in the late afternoons, so after experiencing it yesterday, we decided to stay put.

Off on our bikes to the tennis courts, where we played for an hour. It was deadly hot as we were leaving, and we noticed that Ann had a flat tire. Luckily enough, though, we had just been chatting with a woman who also had a folding bike, and she told us she had an air pump where she was staying. Thankfully, it was only a short distance away, and off we went.

At the house, her husband got into the act because pumping air was not doing the trick, so he and Ann went off to find an inner tube, which they found and finally fixed the flat.

By now, the thunder had begun, and the rain was nonstop. We had lots to do, so it was time to brave the weather, but not without thanking these Good Samaritans and inviting them to dinner onboard *Perpetual* this evening.

We continue to be so amazed at the generosity and kindness of the random people we meet.

We stopped at one of the hotels for a bite to eat, enjoying a reprieve from the rain. It still hadn't stopped by the time we finished eating, but there was shopping to be done since we were having dinner guests.

Back at the dock, there were lots of new arrivals who spoke of the weather as we shared the one washing machine. We were quite beat by dinner time and were not at all disappointed that our good Samaritans hadn't shown up. Safely tucked in the v berth, it was lights out by 9 p.m.

May 8, 1999

The marshes of Georgia

We were up bright and early to begin our four-day trek through the marshes of Georgia. It would be the part of the trip that Jeanne shared with us back in November. As we left the dock, we called her and said we would talk again when we reached Moon River. For tonight, though, our destination was New Teakettle Creek. It was like a parade of sailboats as we all seemed to be heading the same way with beautiful blue skies and a gentle breeze. We passed St Simon's Island and began the many ranges that would hopefully guide us through the rivers and creeks of Georgia without going aground. For a while, we had the jib flying, but not for long as the wind shifted to the north. By the time we arrived at the anchorage, our laundry buddies from yesterday were already set, along with a sailboat from Rhode Island that, for some reason, had been photographing us en route.

It was a beautiful sight to be back in this absolutely serene spot with just the sound of birds echoing so softly from the marshes. After securing the anchor, we feasted on pork chops as the gay men's chorus brilliantly serenaded us, and we toasted our second mate, Jeanne.

May 9, 1999

Happy Birthday to my sweet daughter, Lisa, and Happy Mother's Day to us! A bit surreal waking up in this splendor. This Mother's Day will always stand out in our minds.

It's always a sense of exhilaration as we pull up anchor and head off in the early morning to our next stop. We decided to bypass "Shits" Creek and found a beautiful Anchorage in Redbird Creek, where we treated ourselves to a cockpit shower with only one other sailboat in the near distance. We realized later that "in the near distance" was that photographer and had a good laugh.

May 10, 1999

It was a very early morning, as we left the anchorage at 6:30. We were concerned about a shoal area we had encountered as we entered, and the tide was right for avoiding it. The sun was casting a pink hue through the clouds, and today, *Perpetual* was alone traversing the marshes of Low Country as her Captain and navigator sipped coffee, each in her own reverie.

I guess no matter how many times you do this, you never get bored. That's why there are so many mariner "snowbirds" who head south when the hint of cold weather begins.

As we passed Daufuskie Island dock, I thought about our stay there in November and how much more comfortable we feel on our journey northbound. We've learned a lot, sometimes by trial and error, but nonetheless, hopefully learned.

We decided to Anchor in Bull Creek, a spot just north of Daufuskie and west of Hilton Head. I may sound like a broken record, but again, it was absolutely beautiful as we napped, played Scrabble, and ate leftover steak. Oh, won't I think about these moments when I return to the real world?

May 11, 1999

Off to Beaufort, the threat of early afternoon thunderstorms prompted an early start. As we entered the Port Royal Sound, the sky was gray with some rather nasty clouds and a choppy sea. I pushed up the throttle, hoping to make an uneventful quick passage. We entered the Beaufort River and were relieved to find the chop and wind subsiding and no lightning or thunder. We found a free mooring, and that made our day. It would only be a short dinghy ride to town. For now, though, we were safe and sound, and it had to be "Miller Time."

May 12, 1999

It's sometimes nice to take a day off from the waterway, hop in the dinghy, and head into town for some browsing.

We found a great old bookstore that piqued our interest. We both enjoyed browsing the shelves. After lunch, we were off to Lady's Island to go grocery shopping. It was there that I realized I didn't have my ATM bank card, but following a brief "yikes" moment, I remembered that I must have left the card at the ATM on Jekyll Island. Thank the heavens I was right, and we do have another card, so all is good.

Back at the boat, I broke a bottle of wine as we unloaded groceries. I guess it's not my day. It's pouring rain, and sometimes it isn't perfect.

May 13, 1999

Again, the threat of afternoon thunderstorms is becoming a DRAG.

I was reluctant to leave a safe mooring, so we discussed the possibility of staying. If we were leaving, we agreed it would be early; however, the marina wasn't operating for diesel until eight, and then the Lady's Bridge didn't open till nine. And so, we left at 8:30 and hoped for the best.

It was a six-hour day, after which we found a tucked-away little creek and set two anchors as the alert of severe thunderstorms was being announced. We truly battened down the hatches as the crackling noise of thunder and lightning surrounded us. Needless to say, it was an early night.

A RETURN TO CHARLESTON

May 14, 1999

I can't say we had a restful night, but the good news is that Danny and Bruce held, and the storm was now over.

Today, we would have to contend with Elliot Cut, a two-mile stretch that carries a current of 4 knots with a bridge at the end that has scheduled openings on the half hour. The key was to arrive at slack tide, when the water is still, just before the scheduled opening.

We were out on the water early, had the swift current in our favor, and arrived at the Cut an hour earlier than slack. We decided to go for it and were clocking eight and a half miles an hour. The only way to stop would be to try to reverse or turn around if the bridge wasn't open. Miraculously, the bridge opened even though the bridge tender never answered us, and a few dicey minutes of stress evaporated as we entered beautiful Charleston harbor.

We were thrilled at our record time. We set our two trusty anchors, had lunch, and took a few moments to sit back and relax. The sky was very gray, with some nasty clouds hovering over us. Ann wanted to head into town via dinghy. I was concerned about the weather and wanted to see how *Perpetual* would swing in the current. Ann pouted for a while until the thunder and lightning made their presence known. We quickly battened down the hatches and listened to weather reports of "severe thunderstorms in Charleston Harbor."

Later that afternoon, we noticed *Perpetual* was not swinging like the other boats and concluded that the anchor line must have wrapped around the keel. We both agreed there was nothing we could do about it with the storm continuing, and we proceeded to make dinner. A fellow cruiser noticed our position, dinghied over and offered to free dive and release the line. We thanked him and said we would check in with him in the morning.

May 15, 1999

Woke up to a pretty gusty harbor. We were both groggy since the wind, and our anchor problem kept us somewhat vigilant most of the night. Today, however, we were determined to get things in order so we could jump ship for a while.

After some strong hot coffee, we were up on deck, letting out some line to hopefully free Danny, but no dice. Maybe if we paid out line with the engine going, but as I put her in gear, there was an abrupt stop, and I knew I had just wrapped the line around the prop. Ann was now on the radio to Tow Boat US, but their diver wasn't available. However, we could call a diving company. At that very moment, last night's visitor had dinghied over and again offered his services. Within minutes, he was in his wetsuit, his girlfriend tending the dinghy with a line attached to him and the boat because of the ferocious current. On the third try, he cut the line off the prop and attached a buoy to the freed anchor line so we could retrieve the anchor. We wanted to pay him, but he refused. However, he agreed to let us treat him and his girlfriend to lunch after he had a hot shower.

We decided we had enough of anchoring, and into City Marina we went. We were lucky to get a slip as it just so happened that the "Around the World Alone Race" was finishing, and many of the boats were docked there. How exciting is this?

Mark, our Good Samaritan, and his girlfriend, another Ann, met us at a local restaurant, and we spent a lovely Saturday afternoon getting to know one another. They have been living aboard their boat, *Cameron,* for six years, having traveled to the Bahamas, South America, and Belize with periodic stops to find work so they can continue to cruise some more. Their boat has a seven-foot draft, and they mostly sail offshore. We loved listening to their captivating stories, especially since they are permanent liveaboards and have fascinating lives.

We promised the new Ann that we would find info about visiting a plantation, so off we went on our bikes to the Visitors Center.

Again, we marveled at the beauty of Charleston, cycling past horse-drawn carriages and down streets lined with historic homes and buildings. We were delighted with the bike ride and found out the information for the plantation visit.

Back on *Perpetual*, we radioed Ann on *Cameron* and agreed to meet on Sunday to discuss going to the Magnolia Plantation.

Quite exhausted from the activities of the day, we collapsed very early and looked forward to a good night's sleep at a dock, having not experienced such a luxury in several days.

May 16, 1999

Ann and Mark dinghied into the dock, and we made our plans to visit the plantation. If we took public transportation, we would save money, so we decided that was the way to go. My navigator would figure out the logistics. We would meet in the morning for our plantation visit.

As we were walking down the dock, a man on a bike called out, "Looks like we keep following you." We didn't recognize him at first, but he then reminded me that I had been speaking to his wife on the dock of St. Mary's, Georgia. He was also the mysterious photographer snapping our photo. Little did we know! Anyway, what truly nice people Harry and Carrie are. They just returned from South Africa, where he worked for the Foreign Service for sixteen years and has just retired. Living on a boat was always a dream for him, so they purchased the boat when they arrived in Florida and are currently heading to Bristol, Rhode Island, where they will summer. Harry had been in the Peace Corps the same year as Ann. Carrie was born in the Bronx and grew up on Long Island. Such a small world, and all this we learned just walking on the dock. We told Carrie about our upcoming plantation expedition, and she wanted to go.

That evening, we had been invited to have dinner aboard *Cameron* and enjoyed barbecue chicken as they told us about their lives and their plans to leave for Bermuda. They are heading to Norfolk, where they will work for a while and then head out. Wow, it's quite a different and exciting life, and I feel so fortunate that we are now part of this liveaboard community.

May 17, 1999

All the ladies met (three Anns and a Carrie), and off we went downtown via courtesy van to find the right bus to Piggly Wiggly grocery store, where we would then call a cab to drop us at the plantation. Ann from *Cameron* clearly led the expedition with my partner Ann's expert tutelage since she did the research. Meanwhile, Carrie and I were very content chatting, laughing, and following along.

It turned out to be a splendid day. The gardens were spectacular. The house tour was equally enjoyable, but for me, the high point was laughing as we all sat on a Joggle Board, a board that looks like a bench but is springy and rocks back and forth, resembling a horse and carriage ride. It seems to have originated in Scotland, but Charleston has adopted the tradition. Lots of laughter ensued, but nothing like laughter provoked by the conversation on the bus ride back to downtown. It went like this:

Ann, my partner: "Annie, you need to take a look at Harry's head."

My response: "Why, what's wrong with it?"

Carrie: "I don't even want to touch it, and there has been awful stuff squirting out all over."

Right away, my nurse practitioner hat went on as I was silently thinking it sounded like a cyst that ruptured or an abscess.

My response: "Is he running a temp?" Carrie gave me this incredulous look, and before I could say another word, Ann, my partner, laughingly replied: "I was telling Carrie how you fixed our head on the boat."

Suddenly, in the momentary silence, we all realized we were talking about different heads and exploded into a laughter that could be heard all over Charleston. Every time I think about this, I still chuckle.

Back at the dock, we were very happy to ascertain that in our absence, Harry had indeed fixed his "head," and again, laughter erupted.

We bid Carrie, Harry, and Ann goodbye for now with hopes of meeting up with them again. It was now time to freshen up a bit as we had a date with our friend Michael, who insisted on picking us up.

We had a gay old time eating and drinking at one of his local hangouts where everyone knew his name.

May 18, 1999

Woke up to the sound of NOAH radio. Ann usually awakens first and, since our stay in Key West, immediately turns on the radio where this computer voice is my alarm clock. Ugh, we were out too late last night and needed some Tylenol with our coffee.

Finally feeling better, we biked to downtown Charleston and located a hair salon where we both got fine haircuts for a mere $12 each. Then, off to the Post Office, where we received Erin's Graduation invite and a beautiful Mother's Day card that brought tears to our eyes with its sweet sentiment.

We got back to the boat just in time for Michael's arrival. He wanted to show us his home. We drove to a lovely neighborhood in Mt Pleasant where lots of stately older homes were individually different. Michael's is a replica of an old Charleston house, which means the front of the house faces the driveway. His yard is gorgeous, like an English garden. After all, he is a landscape architect and a talented one at that.

We enjoyed Thai food in a sweet little restaurant and agreed we would make it an early night. We bid Michael farewell with a promise that we would all meet in New York when he visited Gus.

May 19, 1999

Spent most of the morning trying to schedule and coordinate the remainder of our trip north. In essence, we had a "skippers meeting," and we made reservations to fly out to California for Erin's graduation. Our friends Sara and Peggy want to meet at some point. So we figured by July 4th, we would be in the Outer Banks of North Carolina, and that could be a fun possibility. I also called to make a mooring reservation for our arrival back in the Big Apple. These next three months are just going to fly by!

After food shopping for our six-day trip to Myrtle Beach, we met our new dock neighbors, two retired gents who had trailered their boat from Columbia, South Carolina, and would spend a few days sailing around Charleston. Later, they invited us to have a glass of wine on their boat and again another late night. We all get carried away talking. We need to return to anchoring where bedtime is 8 p.m.; too many temptations and distractions on land.

May 20, 1999

We bid farewell to Charleston with the hope of returning again someday.

Out in the harbor, it was brisk but fairly quiet, with only a few barges going in and out of the inlet. It always feels so good to return to the sea after being landlubbers for a few days. We were meeting Pat and Donna in Myrtle Beach by next Tuesday, and it was currently Thursday.

We pulled into one of our favorite anchorages, which we enjoyed so much in the fall. It was again as beautiful as we had remembered, with its vast marshlands stretching as far as the eye could see. Low country and its magical splendor will always be part of my memory. Hopefully, in times of stress or overwhelm, I will recall these days of wonder. For now, though, it's time to just be with it.

May 21, 1999

Today, we headed for Georgetown, another destination we visited in the fall. It seems we will be doing this a lot as we retrace our journey north.

Entering the harbor, we sighted *Cameron*, Ann and Mark's boat, with no one on board, and figured they had dinghied into town. Later, we found out they had been hit by a shrimp boat while anchored and asleep. They dinghied over and gave us the grim details of being woken from a sound sleep with a pounding crunch. They have spent the last few days locating a lawyer as they have some considerable damage and no insurance. Ouch! Since they would have to return to Charleston for estimates, going back out in the ocean was not an option, and they needed assistance navigating the ICW. Ann walked them through the chart as I quietly recalled how they rescued us one week ago. It's hard to watch bad things happen to good people.

We wished them the best of luck and God bless as they dinghied off. There have been many moments when we are reminded of our vulnerabilities on these sometimes dark waterways.

May 22, 1999

I forgot to mention that yesterday, we had anchored again with two anchors, only this time using a newly acquired sentinel that Ann rigged up to keep Danny from wrapping around anything. We awoke a few times during the night to check things out, and I'm happy to report that all is well, and we are sitting pretty in Georgetown Harbor.

We do, however, have another problem: the bilge is filling up because the stuffing box is dripping too much. We tried to adjust the bolts, but after trying, we were afraid we weren't doing it right. The only alternative would be to pump the water out every few hours, so we settled into a night of bailing. At 3 a.m., we were not having fun.

May 23, 1999

Not very well rested, we were up and ready to bail by 7 a.m., grateful that the water hadn't come through the floorboards. We had located a marina just off Myrtle Beach, which would accommodate not only us but also our leaky boat problem.

Out on the bay, The wind was howling, and *Perpetual* was surfing as her crew took turns bailing. By the time we arrived at the Waccamaw River, the wind had calmed; however, we were bombarded with jet skiers coming in all directions. We were thrilled when we arrived at the marina, even with its dilapidated docks and shaky piling. For now, this was home, and it was time to make Sunday dinner. That's something special that happens often on this amazing journey that we are on.

May 24, 1999

The mechanic arrived early and adjusted the stuffing box, so the drip was negligible, but it was just enough to lubricate the packing material. He also changed the oil and tightened a bolt on the fuel pump. I was down below with the mechanic as Ann ran back and forth doing the laundry. We hadn't heard her blood-curdling scream as she almost stepped on a big black snake. Later on, she spotted it again by the dock.

This time, I radioed the dock master, who came out with his gun and shot it, saying, "There's been a lot of these snakes, but they're not dangerous; it's the water moccasins you gotta be careful of," I was stunned and could barely talk. Oh my, as I glanced over at the murky brown water. Ann now wanted to clean the hull of the boat while sitting in the dinghy. I, on the other hand, wanted to go down below and batten down the hatches or get the hell out of there. We decided to compromise for the moment and sat in the cockpit eating lunch as I kept watch. As fate would have it, I sighted a water moccasin swimming towards the boat. Decision Made: "We are outa here!!!"

As Ann was disconnecting the hose, another water moccasin drew the attention of a mechanic working on the boat next to us as he ran to his truck and, now armed with a rifle, shot a bull's eye or, should I say, a snake's eye. At any rate, the snake was gone, and so were we.

For the next few hours, we talked about the snake pit, processing our terror, and were thrilled to be heading for Barefoot Landing in Myrtle Beach, where we could leave the boat since we were staying with Pat and Donna in their condo. There would be no pumping the bilge, no anchor checks in the middle of the night, and yes, no snake searching. We were ready!

May 25-29, 1999

What a blast we had in Myrtle Beach with Pat and Donna, and even though it has taken a few days to recover, it was well worth it.

It started with black bike week, an event that welcomes motorcyclists from all over the country, and what a sight to behold every color one could imagine, in terms of bikes and the bikers in matching shirts. The traffic would be at a standstill until Friday, but it was only Tuesday, so we had plenty of time to check out the casinos, play bingo, and visit the Alabama theater for the Patsy Cline show, where I thought she was appearing in person. Everyone had a good laugh over that. I admit my knowledge of country music is minimal.

The laughter continued at the cleaners, where Ann was attempting to get into a dress that she thought needed to be hemmed. She managed to put on a show for the customers, especially us, as she couldn't figure out where her head belonged. It was Donna to the rescue who navigated the maneuver but not without howls of laughter from everyone. As it turned out, it didn't even need to be hemmed. I only hope we can remember that specific maneuver when we go to Erin's graduation.

Donna's birthday was a highlight as we got all decked out in our party hats made from paper cups and dental floss. Later, we went to the Arcade in Old Myrtle beach and played games, followed by dinner at Umbertos, a place I had visited three years ago for a family reunion.

Hugs to our friends as we said goodbye with promises to keep in touch.

May 30, 1999

Again, we were bombarded by hundreds of small boats and jet skiers. It was Memorial Day weekend, after all. We finally found a small, crowded anchorage in Southport where, after two frustrating hours, we were finally successful in setting the anchors.

May 31, 1999, Memorial Day

After a good night's sleep, we were ready for the Cape Fear River and Snow Cut, and because we timed the current right, *Perpetual* clocked an amazing eight mph. We found a delightful anchorage at Wrightsville Beach, where scenes of the movie, *Message in a Bottle*, were filmed.

We dinghied into the dock, crossed over to the beach, and enjoyed a leisurely stroll. Ann called Erin to find out where we could stay when we arrived for her graduation since she had given up her apartment and was staying with friends. She said she's working on it.

Back on board *Perpetual*, we enjoyed our own private barbecue and toasted to the start of summer.

June 1, 1999

Up very early to make the 8 a.m. bridge opening. Our plan was to anchor in Camp Lejeune, but we quickly changed our minds as we remembered our southern journey in the fall, when guns were firing, and Ann took cover lying on the cockpit floor. This time, we called and were given the all-clear to proceed, so we opted to anchor in Swansboro.

After fifty-four miles and eight hours, we arrived in Swansboro, where it took two hours to set the anchors. Exhausted but still talking, we had an early night.

June 2, 1999

A good night's sleep gave us the energy to hop in the dinghy and head into Swansboro. Such a sweet little town with lots of antique shops to browse as we waited for Diana, Joan's niece, to bring us to their new home that she and Jack had purchased since our visit in the fall.

Again, their kindness, hospitality, and healthy cuisine energized us both, but we had another late night.

June 3, 1999

The last few days have been pretty tiring since we've been traveling and anchoring out every day. We are currently in Beaufort, North Carolina, anchored off the dock with so many other boats. It's quite crowded, and we're just hoping that we can clear our neighbors as we turn into the current. At this point, we are both so tired that we may just put a few bumpers out and hope for the best. Only kidding; we will be on anchor watch. It's a beautiful evening, and the threat of thunderstorms seems to have thankfully disappeared.

We left Swansboro early this morning and had a very brisk day of 15 to 20 knots of wind blowing from astern. The jib gave us a great ride, and we methodically went from buoy to buoy in the Bogue Sound, knowing that one false move and we would be stuck in the mud. Again, setting the anchor took another one and a half hours. Oh well, such is the life of a mariner. Maybe returning to life on land might have some appeal, after all. But even as I write that, I feel sad realizing that in two months, we will be sailing up the East River homeward bound.

Living on a boat is like childbirth; even though there's sometimes pain, the Joy is what you remember. At this very moment, though, the pain of exhaustion is overtaking this body. Good night.

June 4, 1999

All went well throughout the night, and we didn't collide with anything. Sleep was the restorative necessity that helped us now deal with the depth alarm that read five feet. The wind had shifted to the north, where we were now sitting in five feet of water, and it was high tide. There, a few hundred yards away, was one of those beautiful wild ponies, and we quickly realized that within six hours, we would probably be sitting in the mud with the very same pony. The thought of picking up and trying to reset the anchor was very grim, so we said au revoir to Beaufort and set sail for Oriental, where a free town dock was an alluring possibility. If nothing else, we are learning the art of flexibility.

Out on the water, the wind was blowing 10 to 15 kn, giving us a perfect sail. This is the area where Uncle Frank joined us on *Perpetual,* and we learned how to follow ranges. Entering Oriental had a comfortable familiarity, and again, the free dock was open and beckoned our arrival. We were thrilled to be off anchor watch for a few weeks. Tomorrow, we sail back to New Bern, where we will leave the boat and stay with Uncle Frank until we fly out to the West Coast for Erin's graduation. We decided to celebrate our journey and treat ourselves to dinner at M&M's Cafe, a recommendation from many boaters we had met along the way.

The cafe was a charming cape cod house that was packed with Friday night regulars. While sitting at the bar awaiting our table, a middle-aged woman and her elderly male companion approached us and began chatting endlessly about the intimate details of their lives. They seemed to know we were living on a boat and insisted we visit them in the low country. Without sounding rude, we declined even though they became strongly insistent. We were glad when the waiter announced that our table was ready, and we bid them farewell. This was a very strange encounter, but it gave us great dinner conversation as we enjoyed a delicious seafood meal.

June 17, 1999

Here we are, sitting at San Francisco International Airport, awaiting our flight to Phoenix to visit my son, Patrick, and his wife, Kris.

We had a great visit with Erin for her graduation. She found an adorable cottage for us to rent, complete with its own Zen garden and in-ground pool. It became a haven for everyone, including Ken, Ann's ex-husband, who arrived from NY and hadn't booked a hotel, hoping Erin could find one of her friends for him to bunk up with. Of course, that annoyed my navigator, but what really set her off was when he arrived to take a shower at our little cottage on graduation day. Oh my, a little too tight for the situation, to say the least.

Erin's graduation was the highlight, as was meeting her and Chris's friends. Hiking in Tilden Park was beautiful as we enjoyed picking wild flowers and exercising our dormant calves. Off to the beautiful Pacific for a picnic at Erin's favorite hideaway, where the freezing water numbed our toes and aching calves. The Rocky Coast is incredibly beautiful with its winding steep roads that meander through the exquisite homes literally hanging off cliffs.

Visiting the Zen monastery and the Ashram, where Amma from India hugged everyone, was a very powerful experience.

Our only regret is that Erin and Chris are still without their own place. Hopefully, they will find something soon so Erin can begin to practice as a chiropractor and her Mom, especially, can stop worrying.

June 21, 1999

We are currently ready for takeoff, leaving Arizona behind after a fabulous five-day stay with Pat and Kris in their new home.

The joyful reunion began at the airport, where my son, Pat, and his wife, Kris, along with my daughter, Lisa, and her husband, Mike, greeted us with a rousing welcome.

It was easy to get settled in their lovely home that accommodated us all very comfortably. Playing volleyball in the pool was a required activity and a welcome relief from the 109-degree temperature. Sydney and Eli, their adorable dogs, entertained us by playing catch, propelling the ball with their noses. Balderdash, however, became the game of the day or night as we played whenever and laughed till our sides hurt.

I was so thrilled to see my son's workplace, where he has learned so much about surveying and very much likes what he is doing. That's a gift in itself.

It was fun visiting the various model homes that are so reasonable compared to the east coast. I think Mike was ready to move, but not Lisa so much.

All in all, it was a grand visit out west with all our children except Jordan, who was sorely missed, but he will be leaving Africa soon and hopefully be in New York when we arrive.

We arrived back in New Bern with Frank and Barb, and our stay was again delightful. Their generous hospitality allowed us to borrow their car to reprovision *Perpetual* with much-needed items, namely food and ice.

June 25, 1999

How glorious it is to be on the high seas again after almost three weeks. The wind is exactly where it should be, southeast, and blowing at 10 to 15. We are having the best sail since the keys. We are finally on our way to Ocracoke, with an overnight stop in Oriental. We should be there by tomorrow afternoon if all goes well. It is important to have a south wind as the Pamlico Sound is quite shallow and produces a chop with a northerly.

SAILING THE OUTER BANKS

June 26, 1999

Awoke nice and early after a wonderful sleep under the Carolina moon and stars. There is a small chance of scattered afternoon thunderstorms, so leaving early was a wise choice. Our GPS has come out of hiding as we have entered the Pamlico Sound, and we'll have ten to fifteen miles between markers. Our sails are full, and at this moment, everything is spectacular.

It is now 6 p.m., and we are finally relaxing after a pretty wonderful day of sailing the Outer Banks. Again, thank you, God, for keeping those thunderstorms at bay. It was a long channel but well-marked. The winds had really picked up, and it was blowing 20 kn. It was only 1 p.m. We had heard that the afternoon winds could howl, so we were thrilled to get an early start. The howling had just begun. We found a spot at the docks that are run by the National Park Service, which, when we arrived at 3 p.m., was fairly empty but soon filled up with a flotilla of racing sailboats from New Bern.

Here we are, gazing at the Ocracoke lighthouse, realizing another dream has become a reality. This was one destination that Ann, especially, wanted to happen. I have to admit I had some reservations but finally let go; hence, another miracle has appeared.

June 29, 1999

Our stay in Ocracoke was beautiful. The village was very quaint, with its narrow winding roads dotted with small, non-pretentious homes. The beaches were spectacular, with miles and miles of sand and dunes. Biking around the island gave us a flavor of the residents.

Out of curiosity, we stopped by the medical center, a small clinic with two examining rooms and one room that looked like a small O.R. I find it very interesting to see how healthcare is delivered on a small island. The clinic is run by a PA and part-time Nurse Practitioners. He related how busy it can get, like last Friday night when he had to administer tPA, a powerful clot buster, to a man who had a heart attack. I was struck with his confidence, having just graduated one year ago, but when he explained that he had been a medic for six years prior, I understood.

Back at the dock, it's always nice to communicate with fellow boaters who have sailed these waters before, especially since we would be heading off across the Sound to Engelhard on the way to Manteo.

Looking back, I clearly remember when Ocracoke was put on the agenda. We were riding the trolley in Vero Beach, Florida, to the grocery store when Ann and another boater started talking, and for some reason, sailing the Outer Banks became the focus, with visiting Ocracoke a must.

Since *Perpetual* is now pinned against the dock with winds howling on our beam, our boat neighbors volunteered to help turn the boat around so we would be ready to go in the morning. Ann and I could never have held those lines without their help. Something tells me there are angels around us that come to our aid when needed.

Later that day, another Pearson 28 pulled into the dock. These were the same people that we met in Indiantown who confirmed our mast height so we could safely go under the railroad bridge when we were crossing the Okeechobee. Now, they were reporting that they indeed had been to Englehard and Manteo, "just stay in the channel," was their advice.

June 30, 1999

Up bright and early, thrilled that *Perpetual* had been positioned correctly as we pushed off into the gusty channel before the ferry's departure. There was a moment of pause as a pink sky in the morning cautions, "Sailors take warning," meaning there could be a possibility of a storm. The wind was directly behind us, blowing 20-25, and the following sea was big, giving *Perpetual's* sails the extra momentum to hasten the twenty-seven-mile journey. The thought of turning around was nixed as we realized that plowing into the wind, waves, and rain would not be a good alternative, so we forged ahead.

The good news is that there were no thunderstorms, but the five hours of white-knuckling the wheel in the rain took its toll, and I should have relinquished the helm to my navigator as we entered the channel. Of course, we went aground. Exhausted and frustrated, we tried to free the keel but to no avail. After many attempts to radio the marina, a fellow fisherman finally got in touch with the owner of the marina, who pulled up in a fairly large boat and freed us. However, when throwing back our line rather abruptly, he missed my grasp, or maybe my exhausted grasp missed his throw, and of course, it landed in the water, wrapped around our prop, and the engine came to a screeching halt. With another tow line in place, we were now being towed into a long dock attached to a house. This was the marina? For now, it was a safe harbor for two tired ladies who desperately needed a nap. We would deal with the prop later.

It's quite amazing how a two-hour nap can rejuvenate the most weary of souls. The dock master had enrolled a friend to retrieve our line in the murky, jellyfish-infested Far Creek and, after a few dives, managed to free the prop but not without barnacle burns and jelly fish stings all over his body. He kept repeating he was just fine and refused any money, only to say, "I may need help sometime in NY."

The generous spirit of people has been with us throughout our journey and continues to rekindle faith in humankind.

July 1, 1999

There was a moment when we didn't know if we could brave the waters of the Pamlico Sound again, but that was yesterday. After listening to the weather, the winds would be the same but no mention of rain. In truth, our scheduled rendezvous with Sara and Peggy, our friends from NY, is giving us the extra push. They have been managing our bills for the year, and we wanted to offer them a stay at Outer Banks as a thank-you.

The winds were brisk, and the three to five-foot waves were off our quarter stern. Bringing the genoa only partially out stabilized *Perpetual* considerably, as our diet of crackers and water kept us alert and functioning. The sky was bright and clear, and that somehow, psychologically, has a way of making things seem better.

After almost six hours of rough seas, the winds subsided a bit, just in time to pass the infamous Oregon Inlet, where the wind is always five to ten knots more than anywhere else. Thank goodness we were spared again. Up ahead, however, was one of those dreaded "apartment buildings" dredging the channel. As we approached, thinking we could possibly fit, the horn blasted, and immediately, we furled the genoa and did an about-face, radioing the captain, who instructed us to pass on his starboard side. "Yes, we had enough water," was his reply when asked. We bumped along the sandy bottom, but it was the only alternative as sand and water were being spit out of the dredger with great force on its port side. We were now in the channel that would ultimately bring us to Manteo, our destination. Just when we thought we had done the worst of the day, we turned into the harbor to find gusting winds of 31 knots. Oh well, not done yet!

The feelings we experienced, having arrived safely at the Salty Dawg Marina, were quite exhilarating. We had done the Pamlico safely and without incident; well, almost. It would now be time to relax and have fun with Sara and Peggy. How absolutely wonderful life is !!

July 2-5, 1999

Our reunion with Peggy and Sara couldn't have turned out better. They arrived on schedule after having flown into Norfolk and rented a car that brought them to Manteo.

The Tranquil Inn was a spectacular hit, and we even left *Perpetual* and stayed over the first night, enjoying the amenities of wine and cheese at five and breakfast the next morning. We then drove out to Hatteras to watch the lighthouse being moved 2700 ft. It was a scorcher of a day, but we persevered, as this was history in the making and fascinating to watch.

The moving of the Cape Hatteras Light House

We found a perfect beachy place for lunch, where we feasted on fresh seafood and frosty cold beers, and then hopped on the free ferry from Hatteras to Ocracoke. It was hard to believe that this was the same Pamlico Sound that we sailed two days prior, as it was perfectly flat. Peggy decided we must have been hallucinating about "the big seas."

The next day, we all biked to the Elizabethan Gardens, where we found some respite from the heat while enjoying the beautiful plants, multi-colored flowers, and shady trees. That evening, we had a magnificent feast at the 1587 House, where Peggy and Sara insisted that it was their treat. Then, it was time for sparkling fireworks while sitting on the porch toasting the 4th of July of 1999.

The next day was time for Peggy and Sara's departure, but not before visiting the Wright Brothers National Memorial, which was a major highlight for all.

Lots of hugs as we bid our farewells and looked forward to August 7, our current ETA for City Island, NY, where we hope to reconnect with good friends.

July 6 and 7, 1999

We left Manteo with hopes of returning someday. We ventured out into the shallow waters of Albemarle Sound, another body of water that can create a nasty chop. We, however, had fond memories of sailing the whole way from Elizabeth City in the fall and were hoping again for a similar cruise. As it turned out, we motor sailed most of the way and were moderately content with that.

We were now back in Elizabeth City, and there was dock space at the free dock. Within minutes, Fred appeared on his golf cart. "Yes, Fred, we will try to make the wine and cheese party at five, but no promises." In truth, we were exhausted, and even though it's always interesting to meet and share stories with fellow boaters, like the guy who had just taken our lines when we arrived, who had sailed from San Francisco, we were depleted of the necessary energy it would take to activate our weary bodies. The heat was pretty intense, and all we could do was replenish our ice, eat dinner, and fall into our cozy bunk.

The next morning, feeling somewhat better, although it felt like an oven in our cabin. We decided to find a library where we could have access to the internet to check email.

After breakfast at Stalks luncheonette, straight out of the 50s, where lots of seniors meet, enjoy their coffee, and discuss local news, we found the library and enjoyed five hours of comfortable coolness.

I got totally into looking at cars via the internet, something we both need to think about as we reenter life on land.

It was now after five, and we were not going to make the wine and cheese party. Fred came by at six and just gave us a shrug. Oh dear, "Sorry Fred, we are leaving in the morning." It was time to get the boat in shape and us, some shut-eye.

PERPETUAL'S RETURN TO
THE DISMAL SWAMP AND
THE CHESAPEAKE BAY

July 8, 1999

Back on the Dismal Swamp, it was very peaceful and relaxing as we motored gently through the brown water, surrounded by lush vegetation on its banks. The scent of Cypress trees was nostalgically familiar as we once more realized how quickly eleven months have passed and this amazing journey is quickly coming to an end.

The Dismal Swamp

We arrived at the empty free dock at the visitors center but were soon joined by two other sailboats, one from South Africa and one from San Francisco. The heat was pretty intense, and we were safely docked and could cool off in the Visitor's Center.

July 9, 1999

We got an early start to make the 11:30 lock opening and arrived earlier than expected. Up ahead was *Misty Pearl* from South Africa, who invited us to raft up with them since they, too, were docked, awaiting the show to begin. They have been cruising for eight years, having sailed from South Africa to South America and have extensively cruised Central America and the islands. This is their second journey up the ICW, and their current plan is to leave their boat in Annapolis, buy a van, and drive to Alaska. Quite adventurous souls, I might add, and equally as pleasant.

It was now time for the bridge to open. How much we have learned since that first terrifying lock encounter, and it's the same lock tender who requested that "if you ever make it to Florida, bring me back a conch shell." How thrilled and utterly surprised he was when I handed him a small conch shell that we found in Key West. He kept repeating, "I'm really touched," as he looped the line over the piling and then back to us. We were now lock pros as the nine feet of water gushed out the lock, and *Perpetual* was lowered back to sea level. We then bid farewell to the lock tender and the serene Dismal Swamp and very soon to the ICW as we approached buoy Red 36. The ICW had become like an old friend, somewhat comfortable, sometimes challenging and difficult, but nonetheless now, familiar.

As we approached Norfolk, our full attention was needed for submarine sightings and other goings on in this busy harbor. This time, we lowered our sails and motored ever so cautiously, and from astern, there was a black sub ascending. This time, however, the adrenalin rush was not as intense, perhaps because we were prepared.

We found a pleasant anchorage off the town piers and once again set a stern anchor together with the bow anchor since it was very crowded and, hopefully, would prevent us from swinging.

For now, though, it was Miller Time, so we shared a Corona and toasted being in a new harbor, Hampton, Virginia.

July 10 and 11, 1999

We wound up staying the weekend in Hampton since the weather forecast didn't sound good. We enjoyed jumping ship and exploring our new surroundings.

Quite a treat to find an air-conditioned tap room in the Radisson Hotel, where we escaped the wicked heat and watched the Women's Soccer World Cup final on a big flat-screen TV while sipping a frosty cold beer. The whole place was cheering as the US beat China. What a game!!

The next day, we found the tennis center and enjoyed some awesome tennis. The weather had cooled off a bit, and the workout was great. We feel ready to face the Chesapeake Bay in the morning. The weather forecast isn't the greatest, but at least no mention of thunderstorms.

July 12, 1999

Awoke to some bleak clouds, but none presently ominous, so we hauled up our two very dug-in anchors. After fueling up and replenishing our water and ice, we were set to go. The rain began to fall, and the waves were getting bigger as we approached the mouth of the Chesapeake. The traffic of warships from Norfolk was pretty intense since we were on the main shipping channel. We finally made our way clear of those big guys and escaped to the outer edge of the channel. The wind was steady at 15-20, and the gusts up to 25 right on our nose. The waves were washing over the deck. We were so cold, but the warm, splashing surf felt surprisingly good. The bilge, however, was filling up, so Ann went down below to bail. She also crawled out on the deck to reattach our anchor that had been hanging by a thread. It's no wonder my poor navigator was overcome with nausea following. It was decision time, and we decided to head up the York River instead of our original destination, Mobjack Bay. It would be a long trip up the river, but in the long run, it would be closer and more protected.

After seven and half hours pounding into three to five feet seas, we were both overcome by exhaustion. It was only when we rounded the point to Sarah Creek, where the water was calm, that two wet, weary sailors got a second wind to set the anchor and cry out, "Hallelujah!!"

The next two days were spent basically recuperating since the rain never stopped, and the weather forecast of high seas in the Chesapeake cemented the deal. It felt good just to lazily lounge around in the cabin, and we never felt a hint of cabin fever. Our big outings consisted of dinghing into the marina for ice and doing laundry, a big contrast from our visit in the fall when we left the boat for an overnight in Williamsburg. No complaints, though; we are pretty content with this simple life.

The rain had let up a bit, so we decided to venture up the Creek to hopefully find the shopping center that had accommodated my getting a haircut and Ann's splurge on purchases from the Dollar Store in the fall. To our dismay, however, it was low tide, and we had no desire to wade through the swamp.

Back on *Perpetual*, we prepared a delicious tuna casserole on our alcohol stove and settled into a quiet night of reading. All of a sudden, we heard a crash on our bow. A Pearson 26, which had been anchored a good distance away, was now tangled up in our line. Since there was no one aboard, I held the boat off as Ann meticulously unraveled the lines. Thank our lucky stars that the wind was slack as another scenario would have taken place and not with such a minor consequence. *Perpetual* was once again free as the Pearson 26 returned to her former spot. As for *Perpetual's* crew, it was past our bedtime, and we crawled into the v-berth and congratulated each other for a job well done.

July 15, 1999

It was another gray morning, but as we made our way out onto the bay, the sun reared its shining face to the amazement and joy of *Perpetual's* crew. Somehow, all seems right with the world, especially when the wind is up and the weather is nice.

We found a beautiful anchorage right off a marina in Deltaville. The owner of the marina said we could ferry ourselves in and tie up. "The grocery store will pick you up and return you." We were thrilled since it was very hot, and having ridden our bikes in the fall, we knew it was a few miles away.

July 16, 1999

What a delight sitting here on deck, safely anchored with the most exquisite breeze blowing through my hair. These are the moments that make any mishaps or unpleasantness we have endured almost negligible.

We are in northern Virginia on the Great Wicomico River, and what a treat it is to be in such a vast anchorage with only three other boats, all far away.

July 17, 1999

I really didn't sleep well, even though the breeze was delightful. I kept thinking of ideas for the "Perpetual Sailing School" that Ann and I started talking about yesterday. It sounds like such an exciting possibility. Of course, we will have to take and pass the Captain's licensure exam before beginning. Speaking of which, if all goes well, we will be back in NY Harbor in three weeks.

When I look back to this time last year and think of all that was going on: my daughter's wedding only a week away, living with friends, multiple trips to Defender Marine, provisioning and outfitting, *Perpetual*. It was such a busy, happy time, so much to anticipate and discover. There is a certain sadness as we come to the finale, but as I reflect on all we've been able to see, all that we have learned on this magnificent journey, I feel hopeful that our lives, in some ways, will have more meaning and we will continue to meet the challenges that life throws in our way.

We spent a long day motor sailing and pulled into Solomons Island in the late afternoon. After anchoring, I went down below and, for some reason, turned on our little TV and heard the tragic news of John Kennedy Jr. and his wife Carolyn Bessette's plane crash. How much can one family go through?

July 22, 1999

For the last few days, our attention, like the rest of the world, has been focused on updates of this tragedy.

We sailed into Annapolis Harbor, and it was an amazing scene as hundreds of sailboats were also enjoying the perfect wind. It was a bit tricky negotiating the harbor buoys as some had been changed and renumbered. Miraculously, it was uneventful. We found a spot in Spa Creek where we anchored and decided to stay a spell.

We spent a pleasant few days touring the "capital of sailing," which, although bustling, presents a very quaint picturesque setting. We were thrilled to find our much-needed Joker valve for our marine head at Fawcett's Marine Store and some other needed items in the town's hardware store. It was there we heard the news that the bodies of John Jr., his wife Carolyn, and her sister had been found.

Later that day, while visiting the naval chapel and reading some of the scriptures on the beautiful stained glass windows, I was overcome with this calm, almost surreal feeling that these three people were now experiencing perfect happiness. As for the heartbroken families, I hope they believe in something that can give them the strength for their long, painful journey.

Later that day, we telephoned Coleen and Bob and were thrilled we could meet for dinner.

It was great catching up on all their news. They have sold their boat, *Long Shot,* and are hoping to find a fifty-three-foot Hatteras that they can permanently live aboard. They promised to visit us sometime in New York.

We were thrilled to have found a boatyard that would service the engine, hopefully for the last time.

I almost forgot to mention I drowned our only phone as my water bottle wasn't closed tightly. Now, we truly know it's time to get home.

July 23, 1999

It was early morning as we hauled in the anchor with this black sticky sludge that left its mess all over the bow. In all our anchoring days, we had never witnessed such a mess. The ducks also had a field day in our dinghy and left many souvenirs behind. We will have a major cleaning event when we get to Baltimore, a very short trip.

We were among only a few boats exiting Annapolis Harbor at such an early hour and were quite pleased that the wind would give us a great push for a nice sail.

It was a short run to the Baltimore Harbor entrance but another two hours to our planned destination in the inner harbor. The debris and garbage in the harbor were unbelievable, and we were totally shocked. We had planned on anchoring but quickly changed our minds and decided to spring for a marina and abandon ship.

We were now in the heart of a big city on a sweltering hot day In search of a beauty salon to get much-needed haircuts. Weren't we happy campers, or should I say sailors, when we found an amazing air-conditioned salon and settled into a heavenly two hours of being pampered. What a treat!

July 24, 1999

Negotiating phone calls at pay phones is now our newest dilemma. We finally figured out a credit card would do the trick after using seven dollars worth of quarters to make a marina reservation in Cape May.

We called our friend Jeanne, who sailed with us through the marshlands of Georgia, and she is totally psyched about joining us for our final week's voyage into New York. Yes, she will bring Frank Sinatra's "New York, New York." Marie and Carol, whom we saw in Cape May on the southern part of our trip, will again rendezvous with us for a Sunday night dinner in Cape May.

Back at the dock, the breeze had kicked up, and it was a perfect day to clean the dinghy and *Perpetual's* disgusting deck.

Having voiced our concern to the dockmaster about the debris in the harbor, we were happy to hear that this was a recent event because of torrential rain that washed up garbage from the sewers into the river. The event was published in the local papers and hopefully will remind people to dispose of garbage properly. The clean-up boats were working overtime, and it was beginning to look a tad improved.

By late afternoon, we decided to dig out our bikes and do one last shopping before Cape May. We were a sight to behold. Both bikes were loaded with groceries as Ann listed a little too far on a curve, and everything came tumbling out of the "Marathon" crate, particularly named in Marathon, Florida, when we were living in a boatyard. Luckily, nothing broke, and with the help of a passer by, we were merrily on our way.

July 25, 1999

We were underway by seven. We enjoyed a beautiful day on the bay and managed to sail for a few hours. The engine, however, had a louder vibrating sound than usual, and at first glance, it looked ok. It wasn't until the next morning that I shook the alternator and noticed a bolt had lost the nut that secures it to the housing that supports the diesel. It felt pretty miraculous as I blindly searched the oil pan and felt the stray nut. Our guardian angels sometimes work overtime.

That evening, we were anchored off Betterton Beach and again marveled at the beauty surrounding us while we enjoyed barbecued steak. We realized that this was our last Sunday on the Chesapeake.

July 26, 1999

We are back in Chesapeake City, anchored off the Chesapeake Inn, as a band plays favorites from the 60s and 70s.

It's hard to believe it was ten months ago that we found this beautiful spot while waiting out Hurricane "Bonnie." Nostalgic reminiscing has become a daily occurrence as we retrace the waters northbound.

We enjoyed a magnificent sail and hugged close to the main channel, giving the mega ships plenty of room. Before we knew it, we were entering the C&D Canal and, two miles later, the small basin that is currently holding our anchor.

Time to dig out my guitar and strum along to these great tunes.

July 27, 1999

We spent the whole day cleaning and reorganizing down below as our second maté Jeannie will be arriving. Her little bunk had become a holding area for miscellaneous stuff. I added more pictures to our gallery of such and finally repaired the head, replacing the joker valve.

Feeling too tired to dinghy into shore, we happily settled for tuna casserole on deck.

July 28, 1999

We decided to break anchor and bring *Perpetual* into the dock at the Chesapeake Inn, where we could replenish our water supply.

Later, we found the free dock, secured *Perpetual,* and meandered around the small town, finding the library to check email. It was imperative that we make some needed phone calls to minimize the complexities of returning to life on land. Ann will have to quickly lease a car before her insurance lapses, and I am hoping that my car can be resurrected as the mechanic is presently making the evaluation.

Back at the dock, we met a delightful young sailor from Florida who was on his way to Boston. Bruce is sailing a Triton 28, an old

Pearson design, and was very curious about our Pearson 28. As it was starting to rain heavily, we invited him to join us onboard. We enjoyed showing *Perpetual* off, as she was sparkling. Bruce was quite impressed with her. We then shared sea stories.

Bruce had bought his boat in Marathon and, after working on it for a few months, sailed up to Venice to show it off to his parents, only to find out his Mom was in the hospital diagnosed with a brain tumor. She died at home two months later with her family present, and he was at least grateful to have been there. Our hearts went out to him as we were reminded, once again, of the precious gift of life. We lent him our Northern Waterway Guide along with our charts since his were outdated. Bruce was very grateful and promised to return them in the morning before departure.

July 29, 1999

We woke up with the sun rising and had coffee on deck. Bruce returned our guide and charts. We bid farewell and safe sailing and hoped to meet again in Cape May.

After leaving the dock, the depth sounder alarm rang out, but we were safely in deep water within minutes.

It was a gray, eerie morning, and NOAA reported the possibility of afternoon thunderstorms, hence the reason for leaving so early. As we entered the Delaware River, we were thrilled NOT to see any "mega moving apartment buildings." The wind was slack, and the water flat. Our destination was Cohansey River, only because there was nowhere else around to break up the trip, and besides, how could history repeat itself?

Seven hours later, we were docked at Greenwich Boatworks with some quick maneuvering in the unbelievable current. Our intention was to wash *Perpetual* and later anchor out but after checking in with "Mr. Redneck," who immediately recognized us and was "absolutely amazed" that we made it to Key West and back, was presently very nice. There were no drunk fishermen around, so we decided to stay at the dock, wash and scrub *Perpetual* and her dinghy.

We were so tired when all was done that all we could do was eat a little something and crawl into our cozy v-berth. At least there would be no agonizing anxiety that we both had experienced ten months ago in this same boatyard.

July 30, 1999

We cast off at 10:30 down the Cohansey River headed for Cape May, and today would be the last sail Ann and I would be doing alone together.

It was a gray sort of day with the threat of afternoon thunderstorms, so we put the engine into full gear and intermittently played with the jib. Most of the time, we talked about how much we were going to miss this life. It has become so routine and yet so enchanting—this simple, although sometimes complex, life we have been living. We talked about how lunch on the water was such a highlight as we sailed or motored, how early morning perked coffee had a special flavor and aroma that made getting up a treat, how we never felt bored and realized we had rarely been apart for more than a few hours. We wondered what it would feel like as we returned to the working world, perhaps some separation anxiety, we both agreed. Our relationship has endured and has grown to another level. Together, we sailed 3,500 miles and managed to live together harmoniously. Not saying that there were moments that we each have had, but all in all, I think we both have a better understanding of ourselves and each other. This journey has been such a gift.

The sun was shining as we headed into the Cape May Canal. All seemed easy until a large ferry blasted the horn five times as it was now backing out and rather too close for comfort. Ann quickly steered to port. She thought she went aground but throttled up quickly, and in one terrifying moment, she was clear of the ferry and in enough water.

And so we found our anchorage and set the hook, and it was definitely Miller Time. We remembered it was eleven months ago that we had our first Miller Time, having made it to Cape May, and again, we shared a Corona and toasted each other for making this dream of a lifetime become our amazing reality.

"START SPREADING THE NEWS," *PERPETUAL'S* RETURN TO "NEW YORK, NEW YORK"

July 31 - August 3, 1999

The weekend in Cape May was wonderful. We anchored the first two nights and then returned to Utstch's Marina, where our friend Jeanne met us. That evening, Marie, Carol, and Marge, a dear friend of Marie's, arrived, and we had a most spectacular reunion in an elegant Victorian B&B dining room with a player piano serenading us as we sipped vintage wine and ate a meal fit for queens. It was heavenly, but more important was the joyful atmosphere created by all present.

Jeanne is thrilled to be back on *Perpetual* with her own room. The CD player has been bellowing new tunes, especially Frank Sinatra's "New York, New York," as we prepare for our grand entrance into the harbor.

Later on, we all biked into Cape May for the last provisioning. Jeanne is so excited to be doing the last leg of our trip, and we are thrilled to have her with us.

August 4, 1999

We spotted our new friend Bruce as we left the marina. Earlier, we had made a plan to keep each other in sight as we were now in the mighty Atlantic Ocean headed for Atlantic City, a thirty-nine-mile trip. It was a long, rough journey as we mostly motored and headed into some big seas. Poor Jeanne got a rude initiation to ocean motoring, a far cry from her first encounter of sailing through the marshes of Georgia.

We found the inlet easily and had no fear of going under the bridge this time. Harrahs was a welcoming sight, and Bruce was waiting for us on the dock. It was Miller time for us all as we shared a couple of Coronas and toasted to life.

Bruce will be staying here another day, so we made it an early night as we bid him farewell.

August 5, 1999

Today, we would have to be on our A game, as it would be over fifty miles to the Manasquan Inlet, and again, we would brave the ocean for day two.

After some good, robust coffee, we were on our way as the sun was rising. Mornings always feel so good and promising as a new day begins.

Out in the ocean was more of a challenge, which lasted for most of the trip, with gusty headwinds which again made sailing impossible unless we were off to England. Waves were coming over the sides as Ann and Jeanne took turns bailing the bilge, and I concentrated on staying more offshore to avoid any sandbars.

We spotted the inlet, and I relinquished the helm to Ann, having learned that exhaustion can lead to major consequences. The tides were not in our favor, but my navigator did a brilliant job piloting *Perpetual* through the very rough and turbulent water, and Jeanne and I applauded after arriving at the Brielle Marina. Ann's brother, Rich, was meeting us for dinner. We could barely keep our eyes open as we tried to make some coherent conversation, not sure if we made the mark. Ten hours on the water had definitely taken its toll on three weary sailors, and we made it an early evening and said good night.

August 6, 1999

We all had a great night's sleep and were up and ready to bring *Perpetual* home and into New York Harbor.

It was a beautiful day as we departed the inlet, which greeted us with gentle swells, a vast difference from yesterday's entrance. Up went the sails as the wind carried us perfectly with Sinatra's "New York New York" screaming from the cockpit along with "My Way." There were tears of joy and sadness as we talked about nearing the "final curtain" of our trip, and as always, Jeanne listened and then bestowed her own pearls of wisdom, which brought more tears.

Being stopped by the Coast Guard

As we rounded the Sandy Hook, a Coast Guard boat pulled up beside us. Ann asked if we had done something wrong and quickly added: "We are just returning after sailing almost 3500 miles."

"Well then, you deserve an escort," and with that, he guided us into New York Harbor, never telling us why he came after us to begin with.

The splendor of the harbor was magnificent, almost overwhelming, with ships of all sizes going to and fro. Wing on wing, sailing *Perpetual* with the Jib and main on opposite sides perfectly downwind under the Verrazano Bridge, was a moment of pure joy as the lady with the torch appeared, and it was another "moment." As we set anchor in Liberty Park with the majestic lady in the distance, it was now a champagne moment as we toasted one another. We had completed our three-day return from the ocean and had successfully brought *Perpetual* home, one day at a time. We congratulated Jeanne for her splendid job as second mate, wine steward, music coordinator, and, most of all, friend. More toasts for surviving our year at sea, over 3500 miles, and knowing very well that we couldn't have done this magnificent trip of a lifetime without each other and the prayers and encouragement of family and friends.

Tomorrow, we will sail to City Island, where some New York friends will gather for a welcome home, and I will celebrate my 54th birthday.

Approaching the Brooklyn Bridge on the way home

Arrival home

On the way to City Island

Epilogue

It's been more than twenty-five years since we began the journey that essentially changed our lives. So this is what transpired following.

We both returned to the working world in New York and diligently plodded along. I was working as a Nurse Practitioner at a very busy nursing home, and Ann returned to City University. The lingering dream of starting a sailing school and a B&B persisted. Within six months, we went to contract on a home in Camden, Maine, which was ideal for our Bed and Breakfast/Sailing School, and by April, each of our homes sold without an agent. It felt like this was all meant to be. We enrolled in the Captain's licensure course, studied hard, and passed. We were now true Captains.

By June, we had closed on our New York houses and had already moved to Maine, only to return to NY to sail *Perpetual* to her new home.

We opened our two-room B&B and Sailing School in September of 2001 and named it "Perpetual Sailing and Homestay." It was not without challenges, especially financial, but we never regretted our decision to move forward with this dream. Sailing the magnificent waters of Maine and introducing our B&B guests to this enchanting life was our joy.

I had already returned to nursing and spent the last years of my career making home visits to the elderly in Maine, and how I loved it. Ann was offered a largely remote position with a suicide prevention organization in NY.

Our kids and grandkids visited most summers and loved being in Maine. It was a magical place, but as we thought about retiring, we wanted to be closer to family and friends. A few of our New York friends had already settled in Rhode Island.

In 2014, we moved to Wickford, RI, a small historic coastal village, and have been happily retired since. We sold *Perpetual* in 2017 and purchased a 26 ft Nordic Tug.

My three handwritten diaries have waited many years to reveal themselves, and finally, they have come out of the closet.

www.ingramcontent.com/pod-product-compliance
Lightning Source LLC
Chambersburg PA
CBHW071217090426
42736CB00014B/2870